Norse Paganism

Unlocking the Secrets of Norse Magic, Elder Futhark Runes, Spells, Asatru, Shamanic Rituals, and Divination

© Copyright 2024 - All rights reserved.

The content contained within this book may not be reproduced, duplicated, or transmitted without direct written permission from the author or the publisher.

Under no circumstances will any blame or legal responsibility be held against the publisher, or author, for any damages, reparation, or monetary loss due to the information contained within this book, either directly or indirectly.

Legal Notice:

This book is copyright protected. It is only for personal use. You cannot amend, distribute, sell, use, quote or paraphrase any part, or the content within this book, without the consent of the author or publisher.

Disclaimer Notice:

Please note the information contained within this document is for educational and entertainment purposes only. All effort has been executed to present accurate, up-to-date, reliable, and complete information. No warranties of any kind are declared or implied. Readers acknowledge that the author is not engaging in the rendering of legal, financial, medical, or professional advice. The content within this book has been derived from various sources. Please consult a licensed professional before attempting any techniques outlined in this book.

By reading this document, the reader agrees that under no circumstances is the author responsible for any losses, direct or indirect, that are incurred as a result of the use of the information contained within this document, including, but not limited to, errors, omissions, or inaccuracies.

Your Free Gift
(only available for a limited time)

Thanks for getting this book! If you want to learn more about various spirituality topics, then join Mari Silva's community and get a free guided meditation MP3 for awakening your third eye. This guided meditation mp3 is designed to open and strengthen ones third eye so you can experience a higher state of consciousness. Simply visit the link below the image to get started.

https://spiritualityspot.com/meditation

Table of Contents

INTRODUCTION 1
CHAPTER 1: PAGANISM 101 3
CHAPTER 2: NORSE RELIGION: OLD AND MODERN 13
CHAPTER 3: THE ASATRU RELIGION 24
CHAPTER 4: THE SOUL AND THE AFTERLIFE 34
CHAPTER 5: FYLGJA: FINDING YOUR GUARDIAN 42
CHAPTER 6: THE MAGIC OF SEIDR 53
CHAPTER 7: UTESITTA: SITTING OUT, SEEKING WITHIN 62
CHAPTER 8: RUNIC MAGIC AND DIVINATION 71
CHAPTER 9: BINDRUNES AND SIGILS 82
CHAPTER 10: STADHAGALDR: RUNIC YOGA 90
GLOSSARY OF TERMS 99
CONCLUSION 104
HERE'S ANOTHER BOOK BY MARI SILVA THAT YOU MIGHT LIKE ... 106
YOUR FREE GIFT (ONLY AVAILABLE FOR A LIMITED TIME) 107
REFERENCES 108

Introduction

Norse Paganism, or *Heathenism*, is a complex and fascinating belief system that has captured worldwide attention. At its core, Norse Paganism is a spiritual tradition honoring the gods and goddesses of the ancient Norse pantheon, as well as the spirits of nature, ancestors, and other supernatural entities. While Norse Paganism has been practiced for thousands of years, it has experienced a resurgence in recent times, thanks in part to the growing popularity of neo-paganism and Wicca. Many modern practitioners, sometimes called *Norse Wiccans*, draw on ancient Norse beliefs and practices to create a vibrant and dynamic form of spirituality that is uniquely their own.

One of the most distinctive aspects of Norse Paganism is its emphasis on the interconnectedness of all things. According to this worldview, everything in the universe is connected, and all things are imbued with a divine spark. This belief is reflected in the many myths and legends of the Norse pantheon, which depicts the gods and goddesses as intimately involved in the natural world, shaping and influencing the forces of nature through their actions and deeds. Another essential feature of Norse Paganism is its emphasis on community and kinship. Many modern practitioners of Norse Paganism, inspired by the ancient Viking tradition of the Thing, or public assembly, gather to celebrate festivals, share stories, and honor the gods and goddesses in a communal setting. This sense of community and shared purpose is a powerful source of strength and inspiration for many modern practitioners of Norse Paganism, helping them connect with the natural world and each other deeply and meaningfully.

One of the most intriguing aspects of Norse Paganism is its connection to the natural world. In ancient times, the Norse people lived in a harsh and unforgiving land where the forces of nature were ever-present and often dangerous. To survive, they developed a deep reverence for the natural world, seeing it as both powerful and sacred. This reverence for nature is reflected in many aspects of Norse Paganism, from worshiping nature spirits and deities associated with the elements to using natural materials in rituals and ceremonies. Modern practitioners of Norse Paganism have carried on this tradition, finding inspiration and guidance in the rhythms of the natural world.

Throughout this book, you'll explore the rich and diverse world of Norse Paganism, delving into its history, mythology, and practices. You'll learn how this ancient spiritual tradition has evolved and adapted and continues to inspire and inform modern neo-paganism, Wicca, and other related belief systems. Whether you are a seasoned practitioner of Norse Paganism or simply curious about this fascinating spiritual tradition, this book offers a unique and insightful look into one of human history's most enduring and powerful belief systems.

Chapter 1: Paganism 101

This chapter will introduce you to the pagan religion and the terms "Paganism" and "pagan." Besides receiving an in-depth analysis of Paganism's ancient and modern historical background, you'll also learn about the various pagan religions that exist and have existed throughout the world. Lastly, you will
 l explore Paganism's principle beliefs and traditional practices.

What Is Paganism?

Paganism is one of the oldest spiritual traditions in the world. It predates Christianity, although the term "pagan" is believed to have been coined by Christian practitioners who used it to label everyone who didn't share their belief system. The word "pagan" comes from the Latin word "paganus," which means "country dweller" or "of the earth." Over time, the term has been reclaimed by many pagans and is now used proudly to describe themselves.

Pagans worship nature and its creatures.
https://unsplash.com/photos/-G3rw6Y02D0?utm_source=unsplash&utm_medium=referral&utm_content=creditShareLink

Paganism is an umbrella term used to describe various earth-based spiritual traditions. It generally refers to an earth-based religion where practitioners worship and respect nature and its creatures. Pagans believe that universal energy can be found in all things natural and often look to nature for guidance and inspiration.

Over the centuries, Paganism has evolved and changed to reflect the cultures and beliefs of its practitioners. Today, there are many different forms of Paganism practiced all over the world. Because of this, it is one of the most diverse religious movements in the world. It's not a centralized belief system like other widespread religions, either. Practitioners neither follow a strict doctrine nor gather regularly in places of worship.

Origin of Paganism

Paganism is thought to have originated in pre-Christian Europe, possibly developing out of a need to explain common occurrences in the natural world and people's place within it. Historians believe pagan ideas were likely developed in small, tight-knit communities where everyone knew and trusted one another. As these communities grew, the beliefs became more organized until they became religions.

Pagan beliefs likely first developed in Europe and Asia, and some can be traced back to many ancient cultures, including the Celts, Greeks, and Romans. However, Paganism can be found in almost every culture across the globe. It was widely practiced all over Europe, but with the rise of Christianity in the 4th century, it started declining. However, it was still practiced until the 10th century to some extent. In the 1500s, the Renaissance was a period of intense interest in classical culture. During this time, Paganism was incorporated into the arts, music, literature, and many other aspects of life.

Paganism began to re-emerge as a distinct religious movement in the 20th century. In the United Kingdom, the Pagan Federation was founded in 1971 to support Pagans of all traditions. Since then, the trend has grown steadily throughout the world.

Many of the world's major religions, including Christianity, Islam, and Judaism, have roots in Paganism. During the Middle Ages, when the Christianization of the European continent was in full swing, Christianity began to replace many of the older pagan traditions. However, people continued to practice in secrecy, often disguising their practice as Christian traditions. Those who didn't and those who were discovered were persecuted and executed by the Church. Despite centuries of persecution, Paganism has survived and is now thriving again in many parts of the world. Today, there are an estimated two million pagans worldwide, and Paganism has become one of the fastest-growing religions in the world.

History of Paganism

Paganism in Europe

Since ancient times, Paganism in Europe has been associated with nature worship, magic, and deep reverence for the natural world. Back then, the land was mostly forest, and people lived in small villages or were tribes tending to their farms or herds. There were many different tribes, each one with unique customs and beliefs.

England has a rich history of Paganism, dating back to the Bronze Age. The pagan tribes of England worshipped various gods and goddesses, including the god of the sun, the god of the moon, and the goddess of fertility. The most well-known pagan deity in England is the goddess Brigid, the Lady of the Lake. She is associated with fire, healing, and poetry. Another popular deity is the Horned God, associated with hunting and animals. Paganism was the dominant religion in England until the arrival of Christianity in the 7th century. Soon after, it started to decline as the Christian church became more powerful. By the 13th century, it had all but disappeared from England. However, it experienced a resurgence in the 18th and 19th centuries when people began to explore other religions.

Like England, Ireland was also a pagan country before the arrival of Christianity in the 5th century. However, pagans there practice a variety of ancient traditions. These traditions include the construction of temporary altars or shrines, the lighting of fires, and the offering of gifts to the gods and goddesses. They also celebrate various seasonal festivals, such as Beltane and Mabon. Neo-Paganism in Ireland is a modern movement that revives ancient pagan traditions. It is practiced by a small minority, most of whom are members of the Pagan Federation of Ireland.

Paganism was also the dominant religion in Iceland before its Christianization in 1000 AD. It is thought that Paganism first arrived in Iceland around 900 AD, brought by settlers from Scandinavia and the British Isles. Paganism continued to be practiced in Iceland even after Christianity became the dominant religion. Paganism declined in popularity after that, but some Icelanders still practiced it into the 13th century. After that, Christianity became the only religion practiced in Iceland. The Icelandic Pagans also believed in many other beings, such as elves, dwarves, giants, and trolls. Some of these beings were thought to be helpful, while others were considered to be dangerous. Pagan beliefs and practices were passed down orally from generation to generation.

Norway and Sweden are the two countries with the most colorful and long-lasting pagan traditions. Even though Norway converted to Christianity around the late 10th or early 11th centuries, the country was slow to give up its pagan ways. Swedish pagans, on the other hand, didn't accept Christianity until the middle or late 11th century, allowing Paganism to flourish well after the 12th century.

Paganism in America

American paganism has a long and complicated history. It is difficult to say precisely when or how Paganism first arrived on the shores of the United States. Some believe that the ancient indigenous peoples of North and South America practiced it in a specific form, while others believe that the first pagans in America were European immigrants who brought their own beliefs and practices with them.

European colonists brought various pagan traditions, including Druidry, Celtic Shamanism, Norse Magic, and Wicca, to the Americas. These traditions mixed and mingled with each other and the native beliefs already present in America, creating a rich and diverse pagan tradition.

Paganism continued to grow in popularity throughout the 19th and 20th centuries. In the 1960s and 1970s, the feminist and civil rights movements sparked a renewed interest in Paganism and other alternative spiritualities. In the late 20th century, Paganism began to regain popularity in America. This resurgence was partly due to the growing awareness of environmental issues and the popularity of books and movies featuring pagan characters.

Paganism in Asia

Paganism is also practiced in many parts of Asia. In Japan, the native religion, Shinto, is a form of paganism. There are also many Pagans in China who practice Taoism, an indigenous Chinese religion with elements of Paganism. In India, there are numerous pagan traditions still practiced today. In Korea, shamanism is still practiced by a small minority of the population.

Paganism in Africa

It is often associated with ancient Egyptian religion and, more recently, with the traditional belief systems of the San people. However, there is no one African pagan tradition. Instead, there are a variety of pagan customs that are followed across the continent.

Africans believe that ancestors maintain spiritual connections with living relatives. There is a general tendency for ancestral spirits to be kind and good. Negative actions by ancestral spirits cause minor illnesses and warn people that they are erring on the wrong path.

San people, also known as Bushmen, are indigenous people of Southern Africa. The San follow a pagan religion based on animism, the belief that everything in nature has a spirit. Ancestors are considered powerful spirits who can help or harm the living.

Paganism in Australia and New Zealand

Paganism is also practiced in Australia and New Zealand. The most common type of Paganism in these countries is Wicca. The pagan religion of the Māori people is known as the Māori religion. As a form of animism, it holds that everything in nature is spiritual. It teaches that humans are connected to all things in nature and that people must respect and care for the natural world.

Paganism in the Indian Subcontinent

Paganism was also practiced in the Indian subcontinent, the most common type of Paganism being Hinduism. It is the oldest and most prominent religion in the subcontinent. It is a polytheistic religion, meaning Hindus believe in many gods and goddesses.

Paganism Today

Ever since the decline of Christianity in Europe, Paganism has greatly grown in popularity. As people became free to follow other belief systems, curiosity increased about past and distant cultures. This change began with the arrival of the Renaissance period around the middle of the 15th century. The first territory where shrines dedicated to pagan deities started to take off (besides Christian sites) was in Greece.

About a century later, Britain became a Protestant country, followed by the persecution of those who didn't follow this religion. After the upheaval ended, people were free to explore Non-Christian thoughts, including those from Greek and Roman literature describing tales and myths of pagan deities and heroes.

The first pagan belief system to be revived in Britain was Druidism. This was soon followed by other religions, as people continued to search for the fundamental principles of life by studying other religious beliefs from different places and times. In northern Europe, people rediscovered Anglo-Saxon and Norse Paganism.

Wicca, the newest form of Paganism, was developed in the late 19th century when there was a heightened interest in witchcraft among pagan practitioners. Wicca is loosely based on ancient pagan traditions but incorporates many modern elements. After the mid-20th century, other religious and spiritual traditions were similarly revived and incorporated into pagan practices.

One of the hallmarks of modern Paganism is the emphasis on feminism - likely the result of the feminist movement of the 1960s. The reverence of the single Great Goddess as the archetype of women's inner strength and dignity originates from this belief.

Pagan Religions

There are many different types of Paganism. The most common forms include Asatru, Heathenry, Druidism, Odinism, Animism, Celtic Reconstructionism, and Wicca. It's easy to see that Paganism represents a melting pot of different spiritual and religious beliefs. Each incorporates its own set of beliefs and traditions.

Animism relies on an age-old belief that everything in nature is imbued with spirit. This includes animals, plants, rocks, and even inanimate objects. Animism is one of the oldest religions in the world.

Druidism celebrates the Celtic pantheon of gods and goddesses. In ancient times, druids were the most class of the Celts. They were responsible for performing ceremonies, like making offerings and performing weddings and funerals. Druidism is an earth-based religion that emphasizes harmony with the natural world.

Wicca practitioners worship the goddesses of nature. They believe in the power of natural magic and use it to empower their spells and rituals. Wicca is one of the newest forms of the pagan religion.

Odinism is a type of Paganism revolving around worshiping the Norse gods, like Odin and Thor. Odinists believe in the power of magic and runes. They also place great importance on courage, honor, and loyalty.

Asatru is a form of Paganism venerating the Norse deities. It's similar to Odinism, except it emphasizes ethics and morality instead of magic.

Celtic Reconstructionists seek to revive the ancient Celtic culture and religion. They believe in following the traditional ways of their ancestors. They find it vital to preserve the ancient Celtic language and culture.

Heathenry relies on worshiping deities with Germanic pagan roots, like Odin and Thor. Its followers believe in magic and the power of runes. Their most prominent values are courage, honor, and loyalty.

The Core Beliefs of Paganism

Paganism is a polytheistic religion whose followers believe in multiple gods and goddesses. Each god or goddess represents a different aspect of the natural world or human experience. For example, there may be a god of the sun, a god of love, or a goddess of wisdom. Every aspect of the human experience was attributed to one or more of these gods and goddesses.

The divine as a concept also exists in several forms in Paganism. Some deities were attributed with feminine energies, while others had masculine energy. Many male pagan deities have female counterparts to maintain the natural balance. Some pagans also worship divinities embodying both feminine and masculine energies. The balance between feminine and masculine symbolizes fertility and procreation. Pagans equate this to the revival of the Earth at the beginning of each year on the pagan calendar.

They also believe in magic and the power of nature. They saw life as an ongoing cycle with birth, death, and rebirth - similar to how they saw the cyclical changes of nature. Pagans sought and still seek to live in peace with nature and strive to maintain a connection to it and respect it as much as possible.

Pagans follow no universal tenet. They aim to live in peace with themselves and those around them. They seek to avoid hurting others because they believe that any harm they cause can turn back against them.

Core Pagan Practices and Rituals

Pagan rituals and celebrations are often based on the changing of the seasons and the cycles of nature. They can also involve honoring deities or celebrating momentous occasions like birth, marriage, death, and transition into adulthood. While the method of celebration depends on traditions and personal preferences, pagans often engage in celebration both mentally and physically. Sacred rituals and festivities are often accompanied by dancing, singing, and drumming. The rites and ceremonies can include prayers and offerings, which can be in the form of objects, meals, and drinks. Offering these items to the ancestors or deities is believed to appease them and form a connection with them.

Pagans also use the representation of nature in their practices. Air, earth, water, and fire were often used in rituals, the consecration of items, or their cleansing. For example, taking a cleansing bath in salt water is a typical pagan way of preparing for rituals and ceremonies.

In ancient times, pagans often practiced in communities of various sizes. However, the number of solitary practitioners has increased significantly since the revival of Paganism. Pagans prefer to worship outdoors or in the sanctity of their homes - as long as they know they won't be disturbed. The primary reason for this lies in how most pagans commence their work. A typical pagan practice starts by focusing on one's mind, which requires grounding. A great way to achieve this is through meditation which connects the practitioner with nature's energy and allows them to maintain physical and emotional balance.

Building a shrine or an altar is also a common pagan practice. This represents a sacred space where pagans can address their deities and spiritual guides or enhance their spiritual practice. Pagans often erect shrines and altars in their homes, typically in the bedroom or other secluded areas. Those who live in rural settings and alone may create altars outdoors. Pagans decorate their altars with the representation of nature, their deities, beloved ancestors, objects of personal power, and magical tools. They can dedicate the altar to particular causes or entities, using it to leave offerings, meditate, perform cleansing or healing rituals, and much more.

It's unclear whether the ancient pagans performed other practices besides the ones that addressed deities, guides, and issues in their lives. However, modern pagans often do daily rituals as part of their spiritual practice. Nowadays, Paganism is considered a highly personal practice. One may choose to do a simple 10-minute meditation every day - while others will only celebrate sacred dates associated with seasonal changes or deities.

Pagan practices place a high emphasis on spoken intention. Many practitioners believe verbalizing their desires is the first step toward manifesting them. Because of this, pagans choose their words carefully during their practice to ensure they achieve their life goals.

Divination is another prevalent pagan practice. Different forms of Paganism rely on diverse divination methods and approaches - from asking what the day brings to inquiring about a specific future outcome. Tools used in divination include runes, Tarot cards, pendulums, animals, plants, and other elements of nature. Dreams can also be instruments of divination.

Some pagans wear sacred symbols, which serve as charms and talismans. One of the most well-known pagan symbols is the pentacle. It's considered a powerful symbol of protection, especially for those practicing magic. For pagans, magic is a spiritual practice that manifests changes, much like praying in other religions. The only difference is that magic has a physical component coupled with a clear intention. This conjunction enables the practitioner to boost their energy to support that intention. Pagans may choose to empower themselves through fierce concentration, chanting, or breathing methods. All of these exercises have the same goal: to release personal energy into whatever serves the practitioner's intention. Some practitioners use objects (like a candle or a charm) to harness the released power.

Anglo-Saxon Paganism and Norse Paganism

Anglo-Saxon and Norse Paganism are the two most widespread branches of ancient Germanic Paganism. They both stem from the same Proto-Germanic pagan roots and have some similarities. For example, both the ancient Anglo-Saxon and Norse pagans worshiped the same deities and had similar views on ancestral worship and reverence for nature. However, they were two distinct religions. Their diversified evolution began soon after the Germanic pagan tribes migrated and settled in different parts of Europe. As soon as the Anglo Saxon tribes invaded the territory of Great Britain, they started to develop local traditions. The names and functions of their deities may have changed, and other gods and goddesses were added to their pantheon. Their written language (the runic alphabet) was changed, and additional staves were added. The Norse pagans, on the other hand, settled in Scandinavia and maintained most of their original Germanic traditions. This included the names and roles of their gods and goddesses, places and methods of worship, and the original set of rune staves. The evolution of Anglo-Saxon Paganism was cut short around the 7th century when the tribes were forcibly converted to Christianity. Norse Paganism continued to evolve until the 12th century because pagans in Scandinavia and central Europe converted to Christianity much later. After their conversion, the former Anglo-Saxon pagans adopted many Christian traditions, whereas Norse pagans maintained some of their core traditions. Because of all these differences, the Norse pagan belief system has been far better preserved throughout history than its Anglo-Saxon counterpart.

Chapter 2: Norse Religion: Old and Modern

Norse Paganism heavily relies on ancient Norse lore, tying religion and mythology closely together. This chapter will introduce you to the Norse religion in two parts. First, it will explore the Old Norse myths and beliefs, and it will then show you how the Norse religion has evolved in modern times.

The Old Norse Religion

The earliest evidence of Norse religion comes from the Iron Age. Archeological evidence of motifs of sun worship, as wheel crosses from the Iron Age Scandinavia, indicate that a nature-based religion existed at the time. The Norse religion developed from a much older Germanic Iron Age religion. Evidence from the early days of the Norse religion is sparse. However, after the Scandinavian tribes left their home territories and settled in other parts of Northwestern Europe, they spread their belief system. For example, when the Norse tribes arrived in Norway, they brought their god Thor, the most popular deity among the common Norse people.

Up until the arrival of Christianity, Norse Paganism was flourishing in Europe. The British tribes were the first to convert to the new religion. And when Christianity reached Scandinavia, it was already a prominent religion in Europe. However, the Scandinavian pagans were much slower to convert. While the conversion brought many benefits to

European kings, the commoners wanted to remain faithful to their ancient traditions and beliefs. One of the reasons for the resistance was the polytheistic nature of the Norse religion. When mass conversion became the norm, many followers of the Norse religion simply absorbed the Christian god as another deity into their faith. Christianity inadvertently inspired new forms of pagan expressions by influencing various myths.

By the 12th century, Christianity had spread to all corners of Northwestern Europe, nearly eradicating all other religions from these areas, including Norse Paganism. However, the stories of the mighty Norse deities continued to be passed down orally for at least two centuries. While it's unclear how the transmission occurred, some believe the Norse gods were worshipped in secrecy by faithful devotees who were hesitant to abandon their pagan past. As a result, Norse mythology remained popular for hundreds of years after belief in its deities had faded. Despite the prevalence of Christianity in Scandinavia during this period, pagan rituals were observed for centuries afterward. Today, Norse mythology is still important to many people and is a source of inspiration in art, literature, and music.

The Norse Belief System

The ancient Norse religion was polytheistic and concentrated on the reverence of a pantheon of gods, goddesses, and other supernatural beings.

Norse Deities

The ancient Norse were divided into two tribes; the Aesir and the Vanir. The Aesir were the first tribe of gods, living in the heavens and attributed with celestial powers. Living in Asgard, they ruled over war, wisdom, courage, and duty. They were worshiped by warriors and leaders. The Aesir were protectors who watched over the other kingdoms and established law and order across all the realms. The Vanir, on the other hand, were minor gods and goddesses associated with the natural world. Living in Vanaheim, the Vanir were deities of fertility, harvest, the sea, seasons, and love. The followers were peasants who depended more on nature's cycles.

The Aesir Gods

Odin

Odin, god of magic and wisdom.
https://commons.wikimedia.org/wiki/File:Odin_(Manual_of_Mythology).jpg

Odin was the most powerful and feared of the Norse gods. Not only was he respected by mortals but also by the gods. He was the god of wisdom, magic, war, and poetry. However, despite being a symbol of justice, he was also known for disguising himself and stirring trouble among the mortals, which often led to wars. According to the lore, he did this to collect the warriors' souls in Valhalla and build an army for the upcoming battle at Ragnarok.

Odin also was considered to be a god of shamanism and had a significant influence on shamans. According to the Old Norse legends, he could travel to other realms while seemingly looking asleep or dead. Odin had two ravens that brought him news from all the realms and two wolves that served as his loyal and fierce companions.

Odin has often been associated with poetry in Norse myths and has been known to speak eloquently and use poems in his speech. Poetry, or in other words, knowledge, was a gift he carried and gave only to those he deemed worthy. Odin stole the mead of poetry from the giants and gave it to the gods and goddesses of his choosing, along with a few mortal followers.

Odin is associated with death. As an avid seeker of knowledge, he was known for his ability to communicate with the dead. Some sources suggest that he even raised the souls of the dead to seek their knowledge and wisdom.

Frigg

As the most powerful of the Aesir goddesses and Odin's wife, Frigg is the queen of Asgard. For the Germanic people, Frigg was a symbol of motherhood, although her roles were diminished in Norse mythology. She is also the patron goddess of marriage, and the day Friday was derived from her name. Therefore, Norse Pagans believed that Friday was the best day to get married. While some sources depict Frigg as unfaithful or cunning, she was shown in the Poetic Edda to be a loving mother and wife. She wept when her son Baldur was killed. She was always mentioned as Odin's equal and a worthy match for him regarding wisdom and intellect.

Thor

As the protector and guardian of warriors, Thor was one of the most prominent figures in the Aesir pantheon. He believed in order and was the god people turned to when they wanted social stability and justice. Thor was the god of thunder and the sky and, in some versions of the Norse myths, of agriculture. He was birthed by Jord, the embodiment of the Earth and one of Odin's lovers.

Thor was the defender of Asgard and Midgard, a mighty warrior and a masculine figure whose legend continued over the years and passed from generation to generation. There are several myths of him slaying giants to defend either world. While his compelling sense of duty often put him in danger, he never relented in his efforts to protect the weak and those who needed his help. His faithful companion - his hammer Mjöllnir - was his largest weapon, but he also used it for other purposes. For example, he used it to bless weddings, social events, and lands where peasants would plant crops or build their dwellings.

According to the lore, Thor travels across Asgard and Midgard in a chariot pulled by two goats. He is also associated with rain and tidal waves and was asked to bless crops and help people find sustenance. He is said to be straightforward but often only follows his own moral compass. Thor was prophesied to die in Ragnarok, but he would do this by first taking down the world serpent, Jörmungandr.

Loki

Loki is a trickster god in Norse mythology, notorious for mischief and crime. His position in the Aesir pantheon isn't entirely clear. While most sources claim his father to be Jotunn Farbauti and his mother the giantesses Laufey, other sources disagree. Loki is often depicted as Thor and Odin's companion, but he most likely used them for his own gain. Often self-serving and disregarding the consequences of his actions, Loki is usually described as a deity who does what he wants.

Despite this, Loki also used his wit and cunning several times to help his companion gods escape trouble. He was also known for making things right and fixing whatever he ruined, although doing this sometimes under duress. Because of his intellect, the Aesir often calls on Loki to help solve problems, even when it isn't his fault.

Loki is a shapeshifter who can change form and gender - evidenced by the fact that he mothered some of his children and fathered others. His offspring play a pivotal role in Ragnarok, as two would kill the Aesir's most powerful warriors, Odin and Thor. Loki and Heimdall are predicted to battle during Ragnarok, and the two will kill one another. Perhaps the most notorious tale of Loki's mischief in Norse myths is how he had Baldur killed through deception - and later on, continued with his scheme and stopped the return of Baldur's soul from Hel.

Baldur

The Aesir god of ineffable wisdom, Baldur, was also known for his striking features. He settled disputes among feuding gods and mortals - and did this using only his charm and wit. As a son of Odin, Baldur had many brothers and half-brothers, including Thor. He wed the goddess Nanna, and their son Forseti inherited his father's wisdom and appreciation for justice. He resolved conflict in the same calm manner and was known to be a symbol of peace and justice.

Heimdall

As the guardian of the Aesir realm of Asgard, Heimdall lived in Himinbjorg. Ever watchful and vigilant, Heimdall was blessed with hearing so powerful that he could listen to the grass growing and wool growing on sheep. He could also see for hundreds of miles, day and night.

Heimdall was one of Odin's sons and is another figure held in high regard by the Norse Pagans and other Germanic people. Some sources claim him to be the father of mankind, possibly because he taught mortals many things, like the notion of social classes. When he wasn't standing guard, Heimdall wandered Midgard in disguise, advising people, especially couples. Some sources suggest that Heimdall was born to nine maidens, who were also sisters. He wielded a massive sword, and according to some tales, he had the gift of foresight and could look into the future.

Tyr

Tyr is one of the oldest gods in Germanic lore, associated with war, peace, treaties, and justice. Unlike Odin, who only incited wars, Tyr was tied to all aspects of battle, including its ending. His name is associated with the day "Tuesday," which connects to the two names, Tyr and Mars - the latter stemming from Tyr's adoption by Romans as their god Mars.

Tyr was responsible for upholding order and law as well as spreading justice. He was also courageous. This was shown in the tale of the binding of Fenrir, where Tyr sacrificed his arm to ensure that the giant beast was bound and could not hurt anyone. His sacrifice is often compared to that of Odin, who sacrificed his eye to gain knowledge.

The Vanir Gods

Freyja

Fathered by Njord, Freyja was born to the Vanir tribe on Vanaheim until she was kidnapped and taken to Asgard after the war, where she lived among the Aesir. She was married to her brother Freyr. Freyja is often associated with love, lust, fertility, and beauty. It is said that her beauty was unparalleled, and all who saw her coveted her. She was fond of her attributes and liked to indulge in pleasure and passion.

Freyja was also a skilled magic practitioner and heavily associated with shamanism and Seidr. Because of this, she was considered a seeress among the gods. She had many shamanic and magical powers, like transforming into a falcon. According to some Norse tales, she was associated with war and battle. She claimed half the souls of fallen warriors in the battle for her realm Folkvangr.

Freyr

Freyja's brother Freyr was another fertility god in Norse mythology, and he's been linked to the sun and abundance. Freyr was one of the most prominent gods among the Vanir tribe and was worshiped more than his sister or father. After he and his sister departed from the Vanir, Freyr is believed to have been married to the Jotunn Gerðr, another goddess. Freyr was also a valiant warrior who was not without battlefield experience. He's prophesied to fight the fire giant Surtr in Ragnarok and die.

Freyr was often prayed to as a fertility god for a successful harvest. He could control the rain and sunshine, and mortals asked for his blessing so they could prosper. Freyr was linked to masculinity and was invoked in weddings and social celebrations to bring happiness. He was also loved by the gods because he blessed them with abundance during harvest, wealth, and fertility.

Njord

Njord was the father of Freyja and Freyr and the Vanir god of hunting, fishing, seafaring, and the wind. Like many Vanir Gods, he was also associated with fertility and wealth. After the war, he was sent to Asgard along with Freyja and Freya, making him an honorary member of the Aesir.

Norse Mythology and Cosmology

Norse mythology starts with the myth of creation and ends with Ragnarok - the end of the world and the death of most gods and mortals. According to Norse beliefs, the creation of the world started with Ginnungagap, a giant gap that existed even before the sea, land, or sky was formed.

This was located between the realm of ice, Niflheim, and the realm of fire, Muspelheim. The latter was filled with molten lava and smoke, and when the fires leaped out of it, they clashed with the ice growing out from Niflheim. As a result, in Ginnungagap, the fire melted the ice, and out of the drops of melted ice came Ymir, the first giant. The melted drops also created Audhumla (Auðumbla), the primeval cow whose milk nourished Ymir. When Ymir slept, giants were born out of his arms and legs. Auðumbla survived by licking salty rime rocks for nourishment, which is how the first Aesir god, Buri, was created. His son Bor wed

Bestla, the daughter of the giant Bolthorn, and from their union, Odin, Vili, and Ve were born.

The three brothers went on to shape the world. Odin, Vili, and Ve killed Ymir and took his body to Ginnungagap. There, they used his blood to flood the abyss, forming the oceans. They used his skin and muscles to make the soil, while his hair was used to create vegetation. They used Ymir's bones shaped rocks and stones and his brain to form the clouds, after placing his skull over the Earth to form the sky out of it. The brothers then used the embers of Muspelheim to make light and stars. Odin, Vili, and Ve created the first man and woman from tree trunks. They called them Ask and Embla.

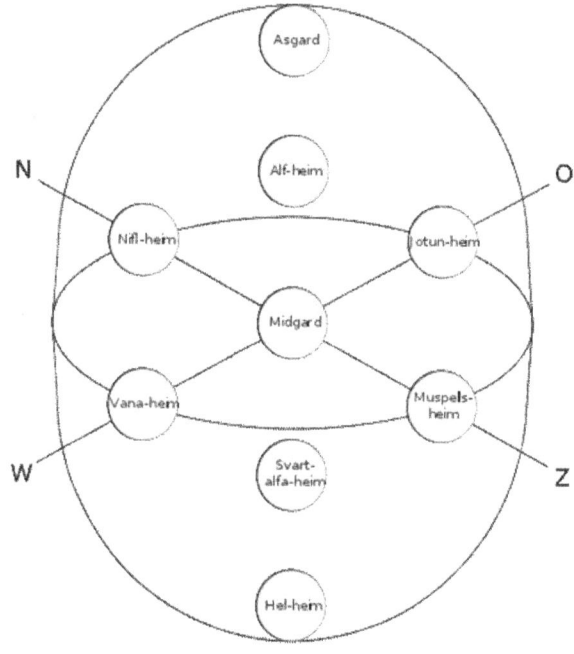

The nine realms.
Et2brute, CC0, via Wikimedia Commons:
https://commons.wikimedia.org/wiki/File:Nine_Realms.svg

In Norse mythology, the universe consists of nine realms connected by the World Tree Yggdrasil. The nine realms are:

- **Asgard:** The home of the Aesir gods and goddesses.
- **Vanaheim**: The world where the Vanir gods and goddesses lived.
- **Midgard:** The world of mortals.
- **Muspelheim**: The primordial world of fire.
- **Niflheim**: The primordial world of ice.
- **Jotunheim:** The world of the frost giants.
- **Nidavellir or Svartalfheim:** The home of the dwarves.
- **Alfheim:** The world of the light elves.
- **Hel or Helheim:** The underworld.

The Norse Religion's Core Values

Animism

Norse Pagans didn't look for the divine energies in the sky but in everyday life and everything surrounding them. According to myth, the deities didn't always dwell in a distant realm. Instead, they took the form of animals and other aspects of nature. Spirits and magic were found in even inanimate objects, like rocks.

The Importance of Ancestors

Norse Pagans deeply revered their ancestors and took great pride in keeping in touch with them. Ancestors were part of the family, and a strong connection with them could provide plenty of benefits. Those who disregard their heritage and their ancestors are believed to be destined to experience many misfortunes.

Hospitality, Hard Work, and Integrity

The ancient Norse people cared deeply for social values, integrity, and order. They found it just as necessary to be gracious hosts as they did to work hard to achieve their goals. They believed that you could only save your integrity if you remained productive and sought to live in peace in your community.

Fate

A powerful belief in fate was a pillar of Norse Pagan traditions, as it was believed that none could escape it, not even the gods.

However, despite having events that were predestined, the Norse also believed in being in control of their actions. They didn't let their belief in the power of fate take away their free will. The warriors often chose to embrace death with honor because they believed it to be a measure of their character and honor.

Spiritual Practices

Most Norse pagan practices revolve around ancestor worship and reverence of deities. Both groups are offered sacrifices and prayers in the hope of receiving blessings. Creating burial mounds for the dead was an accepted practice of the Norse pagans, with the size and shape of the mound determining the status of the deceased.

The Blot is a type of sacrifice often seen as part of private or public spiritual practices of the Norse pagans. It involved killing animals (and, according to some sources, humans) and offering their blood and organs to the deities or ancestors.

Norse Pagan spiritual practices sometimes also involved using divination and magic. Runic divination stemmed from the ancient Germanic culture and was widely used among Norse Pagans in ancient times and even today. The most prominent magical practice is Seidr, a unique form of shamanism initially practiced by Freyja and Odin.

The Importance of the Afterlife

The Norse people believed in the afterlife. They assumed that after leaving the body, the souls of the departed traveled to the otherworld. The spirits ended up in one of the five spiritual realms thought by the Norse people to have existed.

The Modern Revival

Nowadays, people still practice Norse Paganism to connect with their ancestors and honor the cycles of life, death, and rebirth. By honoring and connecting with their ancestors through rituals, teachings, and communal gatherings, followers of modern Norse Paganism can gain a deeper understanding and appreciation of life. Whether by participating in traditional Norse ceremonies or simply by taking time each day to connect with nature, they better understand how to honor the past.

Heathenism

Also known as Heathenry, Heathenism centers on the pantheon of the Germanic pagans. Its beliefs and practices include animism and honoring the deities in ancestors in blots, alongside serving food and alcoholic beverages. Lead by the desire to acquire wisdom and guidance from the Norse divinities. Some followers embark on the path of Seidr. Some are solitary practitioners, while others gather in small groups to perform Heathen rituals and ceremonies outdoors or in sacred places of worship. Their primary values are personal integrity, loyalty, and honor. Beliefs about the afterlife are rarely part of a Heathen's work.

Vanatru

Like the name (translated as /*true to the Vanir"*) indicates, Vanatru is dedicated to the Vanir tribe of the Norse deities. The practitioners' belief centers on fertility, divination, and magic. They treat the gods and goddesses of the Vanir tribe as mortals instead of divine beings. They honor and respect them and expect honor and respect in return. With Vanatru, there are different ways to invoke certain gods and goddesses in rituals, and offerings are made to them.

Rökkatru

Followers of Rökkatru do not see bad events as consequences of evil forces, not even death. For them, chaos, death, and random destructive parts of nature are all necessary to keep the balance of the universe. They don't believe in dividing the deities into "good" and "bad" either. All gods and goddesses are worthy of honor and should be equally celebrated.

Asatru

This is the most widespread branch of modern Norse Paganism. The term Asatru can be translated as *'true to the Aesir gods,'* which indicates that the beliefs followed center on the Aiser deities. They worship deities like Odin, Thor, and Baldur. Unlike in ancient times when animal sacrifices were common offerings, today, devotees usually drink mead or other beverages as a homage to the gods or share a meal with them. The practitioners of Asatru embrace nature and value life, and they are on a constant journey searching for harmony.

Chapter 3: The Asatru Religion

Asatru is pronounced as "OW-sa-troo," meaning *"to be true to the Aesir."* It is derived from the ancient Norse word *"oss,"* which is the singular of Aesir, and the word *"tru,"* which translates to faith. Although ancient Norse beliefs influenced the religion, the term "Asatru" is considered modern and only came into use in the 19th century.

Asatru is a neo-pagan belief that reconstructs and revises the ancient Norse religion. It is a polytheistic belief that involves the worship of more than one deity, and its followers are called heathens or Ásatrúar (singular and plural). However, they prefer not to use the term "neopagans" since their religion shares many similarities to the Norse "Old Way." Many neo-pagan beliefs are based on new and old traditions, unlike Asatru, which solely focuses on old traditions inspired by surviving ancient records.

Although many deities exist in the Asatru pantheon, it mainly focuses on Odin, Thor, Loki, Heimdall, Baldur, Frig, Freyja, Tyr, and Freyr. The religion also involves the worship of giants and ancestors, the spirits of honorable and brave individuals who impacted the people and society while they were alive.

This chapter will dive into the world of the Asatru religion and cover its history, beliefs, practices, symbols, and seasonal festivals.

The History of the Asatru

Sveinbjörn Beinteinsson, Asatru high priest.
*Photograph by Jónína K. Berg, CC BY-SA 3.0 <https://creativecommons.org/licenses/by-sa/3.0>,
via Wikimedia Commons:
https://commons.wikimedia.org/wiki/File:Sveinbj%C3%B6rn_Beinteinsson_1991.jpg*

Before Christianity arrived in Europe, most of the continent followed different pagan religions. Iceland was introduced to Asatru after many of the religion's practitioners moved to the country in the 900s. It spread rapidly and became one of the main religions in the country. However, things changed in the year 1000 after Christianity eradicated all pagan beliefs, including Asatru, and became the country's official religion.

There were still people who held onto their ancient beliefs and who practiced Asatru in secret.

The pagan religion faded into obscurity until 1973 when Sveinbjörn Beinteinsson, a farmer who later became an Asatru high priest, decided to bring it back. One day in 1972, Beinteinsson met with three of his friends Þorsteinn Guðjónsson, Dagur Þorleifsson, and Jörmundur Ingi Hansen, who would all later become influential figures of Asatru, in a coffee house in Reykjavík, the capital of Iceland. After an interesting conversation, the four men agreed to revive the ancient pagan belief. The cultural environment of Iceland at the time, the nationalist movement, and the interest in spiritual beliefs made them realize that the people of Iceland were ready to be reacquainted with the religion of their ancestors.

Sveinbjörn Beinteinsson felt that Asatru was specifically connected to Iceland since it was influenced by the land's hidden forces. He also believed that the people wanted a religion reflecting their identity and would most likely rally behind an ancient belief more than imported religions like Christianity. People were also starting to notice the negative impact of the industrial movement and its ugly side and wanted to return to nature. Beinteinsson found that these elements also created the perfect opportunity to bring back Asatru.

Sveinbjörn Beinteinsson and Þorsteinn Guðjónsson embarked on their journey to resurrect it and spread its beliefs. They wanted to get Asatru recognized as one of the country's official religions. In December 1972, they met with Ólafur Jóhannesson, the country's minister of ecclesiastical affairs and justice. When the men presented their idea, the minister thought they were playing a prank or joking and didn't take them seriously. However, they explained that they were serious and wanted to take this step immediately, so the minister requested they bring him all the necessary paperwork.

Interestingly, after the men left the minister's office, a thunderstorm hit Reykjavík, causing the lights to go out in various areas around the city. The press at the time made a joke that Thor was expressing his anger since he wasn't pleased with the minister's reaction to Beinteinsson and Guðjónsson.

When Asatru began gaining recognition among the people of Iceland, it faced opposition from various Christian leaders and, more precisely, Sigurbjörn Einarsson, the bishop of Iceland. He expressed his disapproval in an Icelandic newspaper and explained that although their constitution allowed people to create religious institutions, they were intended to be monotheistic and only serve one God. He also attacked them for not having a house of worship which is unorthodox for any religious belief and criticized their vague teachings.

The bishop wanted to alienate people even further from Asatru, so he connected its main beliefs to those of Nazi Germany and accused them of having the same ideologies. He put into question Asatru's moral background as well. He added that since it only had twenty-one followers, it didn't need to be recognized as a religious organization. The press echoed the priest's sentiments and declared Christianity as the only Icelandic religion and that they didn't need another faith.

The members of Asatru defended their religion against these attacks and fought even harder for it to be recognized. Their efforts didn't go in vain, and in 1973, the government finally accepted it as an official Icelandic religion. This gave them the right to perform various ceremonies, including marriages. After Iceland, Denmark, and Norway recognized Asatru as an official religion, it reached the UK and USA.

It spread throughout the country to become Iceland's most common and fast-growing religion. However, their priests didn't feel the need to approach people and convince them to join their faith. They believed that their ceremonies and religious teachings would be enough to draw people to Asatru.

Asatru Main Beliefs

What makes any religion unique is its main beliefs. Although ancient Norse mythology glorified wars and made heroes of its soldiers, Asatru's beliefs are different. It promotes peace and tolerance and advises its followers to avoid bloodshed and fighting. The religion also focuses on finding harmony and being connected with nature. Unlike Christianity, Judaism, and other religions, Asatru doesn't have a set of principles or scripture that people should follow.

Another aspect that sets them apart is how they view their gods and goddesses. They didn't treat them as perfect beings. In fact, they are all flawed and have weaknesses and human qualities. They can fall in love, feel hate, get angry, sad, jealous, etc. Asatru practitioners don't pray to their gods and goddesses and see them more as friends than superiors. However, they believe they play a significant role in their daily lives.

Although Asatru doesn't have religious scriptures, it is highly influenced by the Prose Edda by Snorri Sturluson. In fact, many of their beliefs are inspired by the many ancient myths from these texts.

There is usually one high priest who leads the Asatru organization and who is referred to as Allsherjargoði, and ten other minor priests supervise congregations all over the country. The goði of kjalarnesþing is the second highest ranking position in the Asatru hierarchy, and they have the power to perform blót, funerals, marriages, and other religious ceremonies.

The Nine Noble Virtues of Asatru

Although Asatru doesn't follow a set of rules, its worshipers are governed by specific guidelines called "The Nine Noble Virtues." They are a collection of ethical and moral standards that all followers of Asatru must abide by to lead an honorable life. These virtues are based on the Poetic Prose Edda, the Havamal poem, and various Icelandic sagas. Each branch of Asatru has its own interpretation of the nine virtues, but their basics and universal meaning are the same.

Perseverance

Perseverance is the virtue of the strong. No matter what obstacles one faces, one should never give up and must keep going. However, this quality doesn't only involve getting up on your feet every time you face defeat but also learning from your bad decisions and mistakes and becoming a better version of yourself.

Living an average or mediocre life is easy, but success requires perseverance and achieving your full potential. You should never let life bring you down, especially when you feel that all the doors are closed, or there is no hope. Perseverance is believing that nothing is impossible.

Self-Reliance

Self-reliance is being independent and taking care of your needs while remaining connected to the gods and goddesses. Although you should honor your deities regularly, you shouldn't ignore your own well-being and spend time nourishing your heart, mind, body, and soul. Asatru practitioners establish this balance by helping others and doing good deeds without sacrificing their own needs. In Asatru, a community can only thrive and flourish if individuals have room to grow and become better people.

Industriousness

Industriousness is working hard to make your dreams a reality and accomplish your goals. This involves your job and your relationships with deities, community, and family. Think of your Viking ancestors and how people lived their lives. These people were warriors and hard workers who never slacked or wouldn't have survived. Their family would go hungry if they didn't go out looking for food. Although you don't need to exert the same effort to survive, Asatru practitioners believe that one should always have a goal to work toward and keep their mind and body busy. However, you should give yourself a break every now and then, or you'll burn out and won't keep going.

Hospitality

Most people define hospitality as graciously welcoming people into your home. However, Asatru urges its followers to also treat others with love and respect even if they aren't guests. Community is a big part of the faith, and one should learn to coexist peacefully with others. This is a trait they acquired from their ancestors, as hospitality was more than just being polite and nice. In fact, their survival depended on it. Communities should welcome strangers and travelers looking for companionship, safety, and shelter. According to Asatru tradition, if you welcome a stranger into your home and serve them food, you must keep them safe as long as they are your guests. This was based on verses from the Havamal poem.

Honor

Honor involves having a moral compass and maintaining a good reputation. This virtue impacts every aspect of the lives of the Asatru followers. It serves as a reminder that even when your body perishes, your reputation, actions, deeds, words, and how you treat others will never be forgotten.

Truth

According to the Havamal poem, there are two types of truth; the actual truth and the spiritual truth. One of its verses cautions against making an oath unless one plans to keep it, or one will encounter severe punishment. Truth is one of the most significant and powerful virtues. It reminds you to be honest rather than being a people pleaser and say what others want.

Courage

One can't think of the Vikings without the word "courage" coming to mind. This virtue involves being physically and morally brave, *but not just in battle*. One should have the courage to stand up for what is right, even if the whole world is against them. In fact, it takes guts to live by these nine virtues, especially in the modern world. However, you should always be yourself and follow your heart and beliefs, no matter what.

Fidelity

Fidelity isn't only being faithful to your partner but also to the deities and your community. In ancient Norse paganism, an oath was sacred, and breaking it was considered disgraceful. If you break your oath to the gods, family, friends, or spouse, you are letting down your community and turning your back on its principles.

Discipline

Discipline has the willpower to lead an honorable life while upholding these virtues. Nowadays, with the many temptations people face regularly, having morals and holding on to them requires a lot of discipline. You can choose to live your life by these virtues or ignore them and follow the masses. Discipline is being loyal to your morals and brave against the daily challenges you face in the modern world.

All these virtues are connected; failing to adhere to one will also impact the other virtues.

Asatru Practices

Most of the Asatru communities in Iceland remain true to the lifestyle of their Viking ancestors. Ever since the religion's resurrection in 1973, its various practices have spread across the nation.

Offerings

One of the most popular practices in Asatru involves honoring the ancestors. Worshipers usually go to specific sacred sites like an ancient Viking ship or an ancient burial mound to present offerings to the spirits of their dearly departed.

Invoking Deities

A male priest (Gode) or a female priestess (Gydje) usually leads this ceremony. They form a circle with other worshipers to create a sacred space that acts as a portal to the heavens where their gods and goddesses reside. They then invoke and venerate a specific deity and make offerings to appease them. They usually perform this ceremony during the four seasonal festivals; autumn equinox, summer solstice, spring solstice, and winter solstice.

Symbols of Asatru

Many Asatru symbols originate from ancient Norse pagan beliefs dating back to 2000 B.C.

Mjölnir

Thanks to Marvel movies, many people are familiar with Mjölnir. Thor's powerful and magical hammer is one of the oldest Norse symbols. In ancient belief, worshipers wore it as a pendant. It symbolizes community, protection, blessings, good fortune, growth, and fertility.

Yggdrasil

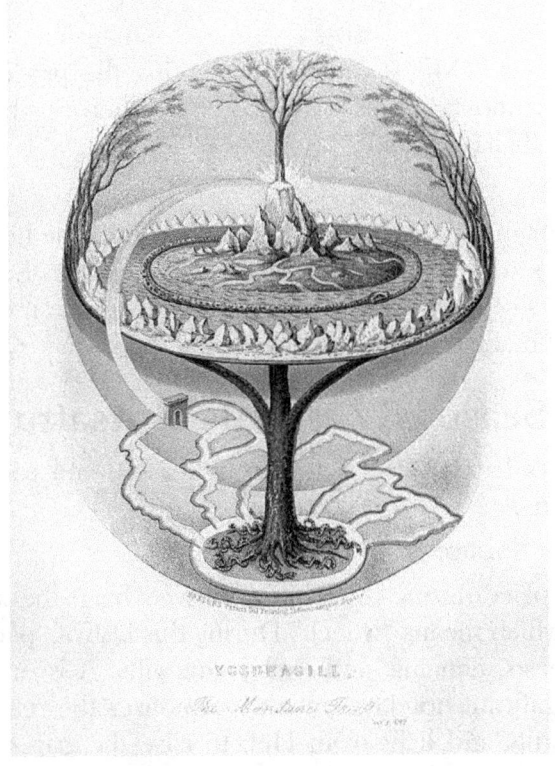

Yggdrasil represents the cycle of life.
Oluf Bagge, Public domain, via Wikimedia Commons:
<u>https://commons.wikimedia.org/wiki/File:Oluf_Olufsen_Bagge_-_Yggdrasil,_The_Mundane_Tree_1847_-_full_page.jpg</u>

Yggdrasil is one of the most important symbols in Asatru and Norse mythology. It represents the cycle of life and connects all living things together. The tree stands at the center of the universe, and all the realms exist on its roots. The word "Yggdrasil" means "Odin's horse" since it was where Odin bound it. According to Norse mythology, Yggdrasil will be destroyed at the end of the world, which is referred to as Ragnarok.

Triskelion

Triskelion means Odin's horns, and they represent poetic inspiration and wisdom.

Huginn and Muninn

Huginn and Muninn were Odin's ravens, symbolizing memory and thought. After any battle, the ravens would feed on the dead bodies, and they treated this event as a feast. This is similar to Odin feasting with the spirits of the dead heroes in Valhalla.

Valknut

Valknut means "Odin's knot," representing the process of life and death. It also symbolizes the spirits of the dead heroes who fell in battle and entered Valhalla.

Aegishjalmur

Aegishjalmur means frightening helmet, and it is the helmet of Aegir, the god of the sea. It represents protection and power. Soldiers used to engrave pictures of it on their weapons or armor since it could terrorize the enemy and make it much easier to defeat them.

Seasonal Festivals of Asatru

Asatru followers have a festival for every season, and each one has its own celebrations.

Yule/Winter Solstice (20th December)

Yule takes place during the winter, derived from the ancient Norse word "Hjol," which means "wheel." During this festival, people celebrate by throwing feasts, dancing, and exchanging gifts. It is one of the most sacred and significant holidays since it symbolizes the return of Baldur, the god of beauty and light from Hel, to ease the grip of the freezing winter. This is a magical time when the gods and goddesses are close to Earth, and the spirits of the dead are able to cross and roam among the living.

Even though Yule shares many similarities with Christmas, it predates the Christian holiday for thousands of years.

Fall Feast/Autumn Equinox (September 21st)

This festival takes place at the beginning of the fall. People celebrate it by dancing, feasting, and lighting bonfires. It symbolizes harvesting fruit and vegetables and storing them for the winter.

Midsummer/Summer Solstice (June 21st)

This festival takes place on the longest day of the year. People celebrate it by singing, dancing, making speeches, lighting bonfires, and presenting offerings to Baldur.

Ostara/Spring Equinox (March 21st)

This festival is named after Ostara, the goddess of spring. It is a time to celebrate the Earth's fertility and growth. People celebrate it by decorating their homes and painting eggs. Ostara greatly influences the Easter Christian holiday, celebrated with the same traditions.

Asatru is a fascinating religion with a rich history and various beliefs and practices. It has remained faithful to the Norse Old Way, for the most part. Asatru still uses the same ancient religion's symbols, follows similar core beliefs, and celebrates the same seasonal festivals.

Chapter 4: The Soul and the Afterlife

Death has always been the biggest mystery in life. Even though people know they are going to die, they don't know where their souls will end up or what happens in the afterlife. Since the beginning of time, mankind has been trying to answer the question, "What happens after you die?" Ancient Norse mythology came up with its own interpretation of the soul and the afterlife to turn death into something people can look forward to rather than fear.

This chapter discusses the concept of the soul and the afterlife and their significance in Norse religion.

The Afterlife in Norse Religion

Death and the afterlife are some of the most significant concepts in Norse mythology. However, there are a lot of misunderstandings about these topics thanks to the media's inaccurate portrayals of the Vikings. For instance, many people believe that Valhalla is similar to the idea of heaven in many religions. However, it is quite different from that.

Most religions focus on the afterlife and advise their followers to lead honest and decent lives so they can spend eternity in heaven. However, the Norse religion focuses more on life experiences and enjoyment instead of worrying about where a person will end up after they die. In other words, people's actions are only connected to their well-being and sense of fulfillment and have no impact on where their souls will go.

This is clear in the nine virtues that only focus on improving the individual and the community. There is no mention that following those nine virtues will allow people entry to Valhalla. The Norse believed that every person is granted an afterlife eventually, so there is no need to worry about it.

Valhalla, the hall of the slain.
Emil Doepler, Public domain, via Wikimedia Commons:
https://commons.wikimedia.org/wiki/File:Walhall_by_Emil_Doepler.jpg

Death isn't seen as the end but as a continuation of one's life in a different realm and state of being. The soul departs the body and goes to the world of the dead to continue its existence. However, it remains connected to the mortal world, which is why the living and spirits of the ancestors can communicate with one another.

Spirits don't all end up in the same place. There is more than one afterlife, and there are factors that determine where each spirit will spend eternity.

Valhalla

If you have ever watched a Viking movie or TV show, you have probably heard the word Valhalla. It means *"hall of the slain,"* and it is the place where the Valkyries take the souls of fallen heroes after they die. The Valkyries resemble their deception in the Marvel movies. They are a group of warrior women who ride on boars, wolves, or horses, holding a spear to determine the fate of the warriors who fall in battle.

The Grímnismál, one of the poems from the Poetic Edda, describes Valhalla as a bright gold place with a roof made of shields and rafters made of spears. The dead sit on chairs covered with breastplates around enormous feasting tables that serve an endless supply of food and drinks like meat and mead. They spend all day training by fighting one another, and at night, all their scars and injuries heal, and they eat delicious food while surrounded by beautiful Valkyries.

According to Norse mythology, Loki's son *Fenrir* is a monstrous wolf who is so huge and vicious that the gods had to put him in chains. During Ragnarok (the end of the world in Norse mythology), Fenrir would break free and wreak havoc on the nine realms, and he would fight Odin and then kill him. For this reason, the gods collect the souls of dead warriors and train them to fight Fenrir.

Valhalla is different from the concept of heaven most people are accustomed to since it doesn't represent the ideal afterlife. However, for a Viking warrior, nothing is better than spending their days fighting and feasting. Still, Odin didn't create Valhalla as a reward for the warriors. It was for selfish reasons since he was aware of Ragnarok and wanted to prepare an army to protect him when the time came.

The warriors won't spend eternity in Valhalla. They are all destined to die again with all the other gods during Ragnarok. Then, they will perish forever.

Fólkvangr

Fólkvangr means field of the armies or field of the people, and it is the realm of Freyja, the goddess of war and death. The souls of fallen warriors are divided between Odin and Freya, half going to Valhalla and the other going to Fólkvangr. There is no mention in Grímnismál about which factors determine who ends up in Valhalla and who ends up in Fólkvangr.

There also isn't any description of Fólkvangr or how the spirits there spend their days. It only mentions how fair and great it is. However, one can expect that it is a nice place to spend the afterlife since Freyja is a kind and giving goddess, so her realm would most likely reflect her loving personality.

Hel

Hel or Helheim is a realm named after its queen, Hel, the goddess of death. The word "Hel" means hidden, and it reflects how the dead and their realm are hidden deep underground. It is a misty, cold, dark, and damp place with a dog guarding its gates. The Poetic Edda states that the goddess is the daughter of Loki and Fenrir's sister. Being a part of one of the most dangerous families in Norse mythology is reflected in her personality. She is a harsh, cruel, and greedy goddess and doesn't care about the dead or the living.

People who die of diseases, old age, or accidents end up in her realm. However, the Prose Edda hints that those who die from other causes could also end up there. When Baldur, the god of light, was murdered at the hands of his brother, he went to Hel. However, one could argue that it could be considered an accident since his brother didn't kill him on purpose (Loki tricked him).

Unlike the goddess's name and personality suggest, Hel isn't a bad place, and the spirits aren't tortured or punished. In fact, she treats them very well. When Baldur died, the goddess welcomed him by covering the floor with gold. However, Hel isn't similar to the concept of heaven since it is neither a pleasant place nor a bad one. It is simply a realm for the dead to spend their days until Ragnarok. They would eat, drink, sleep, and live just like when they were alive.

Some scholars believe that Snorri was the only one to portray Hel negatively since most Norse literature described it as a rather pleasant place. They also believe that he contradicted himself when he mentioned that Baldur went to Hel since there is no mention that people who were murdered ended up there.

From all this information, one can gather that Hel is indeed a good place where the dead have everything they want.

The Realm of Rán

This realm is located under the sea and is the afterlife for those who die by drowning. The goddess of the sea, Rán, rules over it, and when sailors drown, she takes their souls to her world. Even though it is located under the sea, her realm is usually illuminated by all the treasures she takes from the sunken ships. It is believed that Rán treats the spirits well and looks after them.

Helgafjell

Helgafjell is a holy mountain where some spirits spend their afterlife. It is similar to Hel, where the dead lead normal lives with their families and loved ones. Some people have the power to see into Helgafjell, and they describe it as a joyful place that feels like home.

The Burial Mound

The burial mound isn't a realm but the grave where a person is buried. Sometimes, the soul remains in the tombs and spends the afterlife there. The soul is free to dwell in peace or haunt the town and scare the people.

There is no mention that a person's actions impact where they will spend their afterlife. The only determining factor is how they died. The concepts of salvation or internal damnation don't exist in Norse religions. There is only one mention in Norse literature of a place resembling "Hell," called Nastrond, but Christian ideologies mainly influence the belief in this scenario.

The gods don't judge a person based on their deeds or actions, nor do they have the power to interfere with where the souls go. For instance, Odin couldn't take the soul of a person who died by drowning, and Rán couldn't take that of one who died in battle.

The Self in Norse Religion

The self consists of the soul, mind, and body. Simply put, they are the components that make a human being; without one, a person will perish. In Norse mythology, the concept of the self is more complex. It consists of other parts that can be separated from one another. Some of these components can still live on when a person dies and even be reincarnated.

The self and its components in the Norse religion differ from the concept of the soul in Christianity, which is considered a unique part of the self. It never detaches itself from the person except in death. In fact, the word soul or "sal" in the Norse language didn't exist in the ancient religion and only came into being after the arrival of Christianity.

Understanding the self and its components will give you a better idea of how the Norse people comprehended the idea of the soul.

The Hamr

The word *"hamr"* is pronounced like "hammer," meaning skin or shape. It represents the person's physical appearance, and it is the visible and solid part of the self. The body has always been understood as a fixed aspect that can never be altered. However, in the Norse religion, the physical form can be changed. Your hamr can change after death, or the mind can manipulate it. Some people can also alter their physical appearance by performing certain spells. Norse mythology mentions warriors who would transform into wolves or bears.

The word "*hamr*" was used in the context of describing shapeshifting. For instance, "*hamhleypa*" is the Norse word for a shapeshifter, and skipta hömum (hömum is the noun of hamr) translates to "shifting one's shape." The hamr doesn't accompany the person to the afterlife.

The Hugr

The word "*hugr*" means the thought or mind, and it is the first invisible part of the self. It can also refer to your will, emotions, consciousness, and personality and is closely associated with the concept of the inner self. It represents your desires, intuition, thoughts, and presence. Your hugr represents how you make people feel in your company.

Some people possess strong hugrs and can use this ability to impact others from a distance using just their thoughts. Sometimes, your hugr could leave your body and enter another person's. For instance, if you envy someone and think negatively of them, you can make them ill. Your hugr or thoughts travel to the person you are thinking about and impact their health and body. A person can do this subconsciously without intending to harm anyone.

The hugr doesn't remain in the body after death and usually accompanies the soul to the afterlife.

The Fylgja

Look at any ancient illustration of witches. You'll usually find them with animal or bird companions like ravens or cats. This type of spirit is referred to as fylgjur (plural of Fylgja), a Norse word pronounced as "Filg-yur." Fylgja, pronounced "Filg-ya," means pursue, guide, lead, follow, belong to, to side with, or help, and its noun means an "attendant spirit."

These spirits usually take the form of an animal; in some rare cases, they can be human. However, not everyone can see them. You must have specific abilities like the gift of second sight. One can also see these spirits in dreams or while dying, even without any special abilities

The moment before someone dies, they can see their dead fylgja. This indicates that you and your fylgja are connected; when you get sick, it gets sick, and when you die, it dies, and vice versa. Although the fylgja can be separated from the self, it shares the same fate as its owner.

The fylgja shares many other aspects with its owner. For instance, a gluttonous person can have a pig fylgja, a violent person can have a wolf fylgja, a shy person can have a deer fylgja, and a noble person can have a bear fylgja.

Although the fylgja should follow its owner, many stories have mentioned how it reaches the intended destination before the person. Your fylgja can also see and hear things that you can't and uses this ability to protect you from harm.

The Hamingja

The last aspect of the self is the *hamingja*, pronounced: "hahm-ing-ya." It represents a person's luck, but in Norse mythology, the concept of luck is different. It is considered a characteristic like intelligence or strength inherited from your family, and it greatly impacts your life and future. For instance, it can make you wealthy or successful, and it can also act as a protective spirit.

Although it is a part of the self, it is considered a separate entity that can sometimes separate itself from the person. For instance, when a person dies, their hamingja doesn't remain with them in the afterlife. It can be reincarnated in one of the person's descendants, especially if they are named after its owner. Norse literature also tells stories of a hamingja choosing a family member and attaching itself to them. On other occasions, a person can choose before or after dying who can take their hamingja. You could also lend your hamingja to others if they are suffering from bad fortune and want to change their luck.

The hamingja usually takes the form of a huge, strong woman resembling the Valkyrie.

Meditation Technique

Meditating requires you to dig deep within and transcend your physical form to eliminate the boundaries between you and your soul.

Instructions:
1. Find a quiet, peaceful place with no distractions.
2. Set a timer for 15 minutes.
3. Sit on the floor with your legs crossed and your hands on your lap, like the lotus position that many people take when doing yoga. If it makes you uncomfortable, choose another position, but you should be on the floor, not on a chair, sofa,

or bed.
4. Close your eyes and take a few deep breaths to clear your mind. You can play binaural beats to help you relax.
5. Only focus on the sound of the beats, and don't let your mind wander off or your thoughts distract you.
6. Focus on your inner self and shift your awareness from your body and the world around you to your soul.
7. Remain focused on every beat. If distractions or thoughts creep in, quickly return your focus to the binaural beats. Keep doing that until you are completely relaxed, and your mind is quiet.
8. You should now be completely unaware of time and space. You are now at one with the self and connected to it on a higher level.
9. Remain in this state until the 15 minutes are up, then slowly open your eyes.

Norse religion is unique and stands out from other beliefs. Unlike many ancient mythologies, their deities have no power over where the soul ends up in the afterlife. Their view of the soul is also different, consisting of various components that can each be a separate entity. Although many ancient cultures at the time believed in judgment and gave their deities power over how and where they spent the afterlife, the Norse had a different perception. As a result, to this day, it remains one of the most fascinating religions in the world.

Chapter 5: Fylgja: Finding Your Guardian

In a land long ago, a young man eagerly awaited the grand party of the year. Each day, he counted down the hours and anticipated the festivities to come. Little did he know, however, that a wicked witch was plotting his demise on that very night.

Thankfully, the man's fylgja was aware of the danger. It tried to warn him through vivid dreams for five nights, but he remained oblivious to its messages. As the event approached, he remained clueless about the signs his fylgja was sending him.

With time running out, the fylgja took matters into its own hands. It made the young man ill, preventing him from attending the party and unknowingly saving his life.

Such is the power of the fylgja - a guardian spirit that will go to any length to protect those under its care. Sadly, many remain unaware of their existence and miss the daily messages they send. Discovering and bonding with your fylgja, however, can transform your life in ways beyond your imagination.

Discovering and bonding with your fylgja can profoundly impact your life, but the journey to connect with your guardian spirit can be challenging. Thankfully, this chapter offers practical techniques to help you establish a relationship with your spirit guide.

Meditation can help you connect with your fylgja.
https://unsplash.com/photos/ie8WW5KUx3o?utm_source=unsplash&utm_medium=referral&utm_content=creditShareLink

Through meditation, visualization, and other methods, you can learn to recognize and communicate with your fylgja. By honing your intuition and opening yourself up to the messages it sends, you can tap into the wisdom and guidance of your guardian spirit.

Whether you seek protection, clarity, or simply a deeper connection with the spiritual realm, the techniques presented in this chapter can help you forge a bond with your fylgja and unlock its full potential.

Meditation Technique

Tools:
- White sage
- Pen and paper

Instructions:
1. Before you begin, set the intention that you are performing this meditation technique to connect with your spirit guide. You can say something like, *"I am taking a journey to the spirit world to connect with my guardian."*
2. Prepare a sacred space for meditation. Cleanse it by burning white sage and letting the smoke purify it.
3. Move around the room and call on the four directions (north, south, east, and west).

4. Then, honor the four elements, Earth, Water, Air, and Fire, and honor the Spirit as well.
5. Say, *"I call on the Earth's energy to keep me grounded while I head to the invisible realms and connect with my spirit guide."*
6. *"I call on the Water's energy, praying that its currents flow easily and open the pathway that will take me to my spirit guide."*
7. *"I call on the Air's energy to bring the light and bestow upon me the gift of clarity so I can trust my intuition while I journey to meet my spirit guide."*
8. *"I call on the Fire's energy to illuminate my path in the invisible realms while I connect with my spirit guide."*
9. *"I call on the Spirit's energy, Grandmother Moon, Grandfather Sun, my dear ancestors, and all other helpful spirits who can hear me. Protect me and keep me safe while I head to the invisible realms and connect with my spirit guide."*
10. Write on the piece of paper all the questions you want to ask your spirit guide.
11. Now, prepare yourself for meditation.
12. Sit in the sacred space in the lotus position.
13. Breathe in and out slowly and deeply for one or two minutes, and feel your body relax with every breath.
14. Clear your mind and only focus on the present moment.
15. Repeat your intention again under your breath.
16. Close your eyes and visualize yourself standing in the middle of a big forest with beautiful scenery all around you. Take in your surroundings.
17. Wherever you look, you see colorful flowers and tall green trees.
18. A pathway in front of you will take you to your spirit guide.
19. You walk towards it.
20. You feel the air in your hair and the warm sunlight on your skin.

21. While walking on the pathway, you feel a sense of tranquility washing over you. You feel joyful because you know who is waiting for you on the other side.
22. You see the wind blowing through the trees, and you see that you are almost there.
23. You feel the protection of the four elements.
24. You can't wait to finally meet your guardian and have all your questions answered.
25. You have finally arrived at your destination and see a big ball of white light.
26. You walk closer and step into it.
27. Now, you are standing before your spirit guide.
28. Look closer to see the figure standing in front of you. It could be a bird, an animal, or a ball of energy. Whatever appears in front of you is your guardian.
29. Ask, *"Are you my spirit guide?"* and wait for an answer.
30. Ask, *"What's your name?"*
31. Whatever name they give you, use it to address them.
32. Now, your spirit guide will tell you,

    "From the day you were born, I have been by your side. You are never on your own; I am always with you, guiding, helping, and protecting you."

33. You are overwhelmed by emotions knowing that you aren't alone and feel connected to them.
34. You walk toward them and hug them.
35. Now, you will ask them all the questions you have prepared before the meditation. Don't hold back, and ask anything that comes to mind. Your spirit guide is there to help you and will do everything in its power to give you the answers you seek.
36. After you have finished asking your questions, tell them that you are leaving but that you'll meet again. Your spirit guide will tell you, "Even though you can't always see me, I am constantly walking beside you. Whenever you need me, just call out to me."

37. Give them another hug and express your gratitude for all their help.
38. Return to the same road by exiting through the ball of light and walking back on the same pathway.
39. You feel content and at peace after this spiritual experience and the knowledge that your spirit guide will always keep you safe.
40. When you are ready to exit the meditation, take a few deep breaths, then open your eyes.
41. Be on the lookout for signs because your spirit guide will send you messages through songs, animals, symbols, etc., so keep your eyes and ears open.

Focus on Your Dreams

Pay attention to everything you see in your dreams because your guardian can either reveal itself to you or send you messages in the dream world.

Instructions:

1. When you lie in bed before you drift to sleep, ask your guardian to reveal him/herself to you in your dream. You can say, "Guardian who always looks out for me and serves my best interest, please visit me in my dreams tonight. I am prepared to receive your wisdom and grateful for your constant guidance and support. I promise to remember my dream when I wake up in the morning."
2. Keep repeating the intention until you fall asleep. Leave a notebook and pen by your side so you can write down your dream as soon as you wake up.
3. The next morning, write down everything you remember, even the details you think are irrelevant or unimportant.
4. After you have finished, read everything you wrote and analyze all the signs and symbols to figure out who your spirit guide is and what it is trying to communicate to you.

Scrying

Scrying, also called crystal gazing, is a divination practice that originated in ancient Persia. It involves staring at a crystal ball, mirror, water, or any reflective surface to receive the answers you seek.

Tools:
- A bowl of water (preferably a dark bowl since it will make it easy for you to concentrate)
- Table
- A crystal (preferably crystal quartz)
- Matches or a lighter
- 2 candles
- White sage

Instructions:
1. Choose a place for scrying. You can do it indoors or outdoors, but it has to be dark. If you practice indoors, turn off the light and shut the curtains. If you practice outdoors, do it at night.
2. Place the bowl of water on the table, then drop the crystal in it.
3. Cleanse your space using white sage.
4. Light the candles, then place them on either side of the bowl. The flames should reflect on the water's surface.
5. Enter into a trance state by meditating while focusing on your breathing and listening to soft music.
6. Begin scrying when you feel focused, relaxed, and at peace.
7. Sit comfortably, gaze into the bowl of water, and relax your eyes.
8. Focus on the crystal to prevent your eyes from wandering off.
9. Remain calm and be patient. Scrying isn't easy and can take a while to master.
10. Repeat the intention of finding your spirit guide to yourself.
11. Keep your eyes and face relaxed.
12. Take deep breaths from your stomach.

13. You'll begin to see images coming and going, don't hold on to them, as this will only make the process harder. Allow them and the emotions that accompany them to come and go freely.
14. It is normal for your mind to wander off, don't force it to come back. Just make sure that your eyes are focused on the water bowl.
15. You can start seeing an image, word, or scene playing out.
16. When you have finished, contemplate what you saw for a few minutes.
17. You may not find your spirit or animal guide right away. Scrying takes time and practice, so do it as often as possible until you find your guardian.
18. You can use any other reflective image like fire, oil, wax, clouds, smoke, crystal, or look into someone's eye. Choose the method you feel drawn to the most.

Animal Oracle Cards

Using animal oracle cards is a quick and sure way to find your guardian animal.

Instructions:
1. Connect with the cards by carrying them around wherever you go for a few days, or play with them at every chance you get. Introduce them to your energy by constantly touching and using them. This will make working with them easier and give you accurate results.
2. Set the intention of what you hope the cards reveal to you. You can say, *"I want the cards to reveal my guardian animal to me."*
3. Take a few deep and slow breaths and focus on the present moment and your intention.
4. Shuffle the deck seven times or more until you feel your energy has merged with the cards' energy.
5. Spread the cards face down, and place your hands over them.
6. Once you feel pulled to a card, pick it up. This is the card that will reveal to you your guardian animal.

7. Look at the card to identify your guardian animal.
8. Sit with it for a few minutes to try to connect with the card and get acquainted with your spirit animal.
9. Write down in your journal how the card makes you feel.

You can also meditate on the card.

Instructions:
1. Sit comfortably in a quiet room with no distractions.
2. Hold the card in your hand.
3. Close your eyes and take a few deep breaths.
4. Feel your body relax with every breath you take.
5. Clear your mind and be present in the moment.
6. Visualize the card and get lost in your imagination.
7. Observe all the details you see in the visualization. Notice all the symbols you see since your guardian animal can send you messages through your meditation.
8. Try to understand the message they are trying to send to you.
9. After you have finished, express your gratitude for what you received from your spirit guide.
10. Take a few deep breaths, then slowly open your eyes.

Bibliomancy

Bibliomancy is another ancient divination technique that involves finding the answers you seek in a book that calls to you. It is one of the oldest divination methods, and many people still use it to find their spirit guide.

Instructions:
1. Stand in front of your book collection. If you don't have one, go to a bookstore or your local library.
2. Close your eyes and set an intention that you want to find your spirit guide in one of these books.
3. Move your hands over the books and let your intuition guide you; the book will call to you.
4. Once you feel the urge to pick up a book, do it.
5. Open your eyes and randomly open the book and take a quick look. You can find a word or a picture that reveals your

guardian to you.

6. You can also wait a few minutes before opening the book for a page number to come to you, then open it and read it.
7. Bibliomancy may not work the first time you try it, especially if you aren't connected to your intuition. Keep practicing until you feel like a book is pulling you in.
8. Sometimes, your spirit guide will not give you a clear sign and just send you a clue. Use it and keep searching and exploring until you figure it out.

Vision Quest

Instructions:

1. After you wake up in the morning, perform a simple meditation.
2. Sit in a comfortable position in a quiet room.
3. Close your eyes and take a few deep breaths.
4. Ask your spirit animal to show themselves to you by sending signs or clues.
5. Keep your eyes open for messages throughout the day. Your guardian animal can show you symbols that reveal their identity to you or just give you hints. For instance, if it is a bird, you can see feathers everywhere you go or hear birds chirping.
6. Your guardian animal can also directly show you who they are. For instance, if it is a wolf, you'll see images or videos of wolves everywhere online, in books, on street art, or a friend will randomly mention the animal to you or buy you a pendant in the shape of a wolf.
7. Do this meditation every morning. At night, write down all the signs you saw during the day.
8. If you see more than one animal, focus on the one you see the most.
9. Remember, when your guardian animal decides to reveal itself to you, it will keep sending you messages and signs until you finally take notice.

Nature

Your spirit guide is most likely an animal or a bird, so it will use natural elements to reveal itself to you. Even when you discover your fylgia, you can use nature whenever you want to connect with it or ask a question.

Instructions:
1. Find a place in nature like a lake, stream, or park.
2. Stare at the trees, flowers, water, clouds, moon, etc., and try to see a face.
3. If you see the face of an animal that has been appearing to you a lot lately, it could be your animal guide.

Repeated Signs

The universe usually sends you messages through repetitive signs like symbols, names, or numbers. Your spirit guides can also send messages or reveal themselves to you by repeating the same sign repeatedly until you notice.

Instructions:
1. Set a clear intention either out loud or internally, or say a prayer like

    "Dear (mention the name of the Norse deity of your choice or call on the spirits of your ancestors), I implore you to help me find my spirit guide. Please, send me signals, signs, or symbols every day. Thank you."

2. Keep your eyes open every day for repetitive and unusual objects, places, symbols, names, or numbers that appear to you.
3. Write them down and after a week, reflect on them and try to decipher their meaning.

Release Your Worries to Your Spirit Guide

If you are struggling to make a decision or looking for a solution to a problem, release your worries to your spirit guide.

Instructions:
1. Sit in a quiet space and clear your thoughts.

2. Repeat this mantra *"I am releasing (name the issue) to my spirit guide so they can help me find a solution."*
3. Be on the lookout for messages or signs they will send you to help you with your problem.

Sometimes, you can try everything, but your fylgia won't reveal itself to you. This doesn't mean that it is refusing to connect with you. It just wants you to keep searching because there is a lesson for you on this journey. Don't give up. Eventually, you'll find your fylgia. In other cases, its messages or symbols can be so clear and loud that it will be impossible to miss them. Keep your eyes open.

Once you find your guardian, seek their help and guidance whenever you face a problem. Understand their messages and warnings because they can save your life. Constantly express your gratitude to them to show your appreciation for all their help.

Chapter 6: The Magic of Seidr

Seidr is a common spiritual and shamanic practice in Norse Paganism and is mainly concerned with fate. It was used to uncover the nuances of fate and, if necessary, subtly change them however the practitioner wanted. According to ancient lore, the practice was used for both good and evil purposes. While practitioners of Seidr were notorious for casting curses on people, they also cast protective spells and provided charms for empowerment and spiritual protection.

Seidr was mainly practiced by women.
https://unsplash.com/photos/ZOxkaXFvw6A?utm_source=unsplash&utm_medium=referral&utm_content=creditShareLink

Traditionally associated with the goddess Freyja, Seidr was mainly practiced by women. These women were highly respected members of their communities, unlike male practitioners, who were often ridiculed and labeled effeminate. The mystery associated with Seidr was a feminine trait in Norse traditions and culture. Because of this, men who practiced Seidr were thought to be breaking gender norms. Even the mighty god Odin (believed to be the most skillful Seidr practitioner amongst the deities) was mocked for using what was considered feminine powers. However, many male practitioners idolized him due to his other masculine characteristics.

This chapter will explore the concepts of Seidr and the Völva and help you to understand the different levels of trance a shaman can reach. Then, you'll find a step-by-step guide to going on a safe Seidr journey.

Before You Start

It is necessary to emphasize that Norse Shamanism, or any other shamanic practice, is safer for beginners when practiced with an experienced guide. If you're a solitary practitioner, you should gain experience in trance and journeying methods before proceeding to higher levels. Shamanic practices can harm your mental well-being if you aren't adequately prepared or have psychological issues. When you enter into a trance, you'll receive messages in the form of auditory or visual signs. This can be overwhelming even if you don't have mental health issues. It may take some time to get used to the messages and learn how to decipher them. If you feel overwhelmed or have symptoms like severe anxiety and hallucinations during or after your practice, you should stop and seek help from a mental health professional. Similarly, if you're already struggling with mental health issues, don't start practicing Seidr (or any other form of shamanism) until you've addressed them.

What Is Shamanism?

Shamanism is a spiritual practice that involves gaining knowledge or powers through a trance-like state. The abilities you could obtain in this state include divination, healing, or guidance for the living or dead.

The term "shamanism" originates from the Manchu-Tungus word saman and can be translated to _"the one who knows."_ Historical records suggest that it was widespread among ancient tribes in Africa, the Arctic, Australia, Asia, and America. Shamanism was typically practiced by hunting and gathering communities.

While it's unclear when the ancient Germanic tribes adopted shamanism into their practices, myths suggest they weren't strangers to it. Odin, the king of the Germanic gods, was a well-known shaman, and he practiced Seidr after he learned from the goddess Freyja. Some sources suggest that Odin's name can be translated as *"the master of inspiration"* or *"the master of ecstasy."* His shamanic journeys are documented in several myths, sagas, and poems, including a famous Eddic poem named "Baldur's Dreams." It describes Odin traveling to the underworld after the death of his son Baldur. He used the trance to ride Sleipnir, his eight-legged horse, and cross the divide between the realms. There, he asked a dead seeress for advice on how to revive Baldur.

Odin's two ravens, Hugin and Munin, are believed to have been familiar spirit companions, which is typical for those practicing shamanism. A shaman must die and be reborn to gain the power of entering a trance - which Odin did during his trial at the Tree of Life.

According to legend, Odin ignited battles among tribes to collect the fiercest warriors' souls. Some of the warriors he selected were also suggested to have the ability to practice Seidr or another form of shamanism. According to the Ynglinga Saga, some of Odin's warriors went into battle as if in a trance. They acted like animals and didn't wear any armor. They couldn't be harmed, and they constantly won battles. This indicates that they became possessed by the spirits of animals. Other sources describe these warriors shifting their shapes to become wolves and bears.

What Is Seidr?

Seidr is an ancient form of Norse shamanism. Besides trances, it also relies on magic to foretell fate, identify one's purpose in life, and manipulate fate to create desired changes. Practitioners did all of this by using trances and magic to symbolically weave the threads of fate in a way that they attract desired situations and events. Their rituals and ceremonies typically began with them entering a trance where they would communicate with the spirit world and harness its wisdom. Their purposes included casting curses or blessings, bringing empowerment and protection, or a prophecy about future events.

Seidr rituals were also used for clairvoyance, an approach that allowed the practitioner to locate hidden objects or thoughts. It was also used to attract abundance and good luck, ensure a good harvest, and hunt by controlling the weather and conjuring animals. When used for malicious purposes, Seidr was used to induce sickness, make a land barren, or prevent an enemy from winning in battle. Instead of curses, the practitioner could also tell people false prophecies to lead them toward the wrong path. Due to these false readings, practitioners could make people injure and kill their adversaries, whether in a battle or in a simple disagreement. Those who mastered the art of weaving or changing fate were known as the Norns. They were said to be the first and most proficient practitioners.

The god Odin and the goddess Freya are two significant Vanir and Aesir deities who mastered the art of Seidr. As the divine archetypes of male and female practitioners, their duality plays a unique role in a gendered practice like Seidr.

What Is a Völva?

The goddess Freyja was thought to serve as a role model for Völva - a female practitioner of Seidr. According to Norse lore, Freyja was the first deity to bring the practice of Seidr to the realm of the gods. Due to their healing powers and ability to perform magic and provide spiritual guidance, a Völva was a highly respected member of their community. Being a leading figure herself, a Völva was usually respected and protected by their clan or tribe's leaders. Male Seidr practitioners were called seers, but they were much rarer.

A Völva roamed the towns and performed magic in return for several forms of compensation, including room and board. Many sagas and heroic poems (most notably: The Saga of Erik the Red, and The Insight of the Völva, respectively) offer detailed descriptions of a Völva and her practices.

Even though they were treated with respect, Völvas were often segregated from society. This had both negative and positive connotations. On one hand, a Völva was feared and often stigmatized because they could cast powerful curses. They also led nomadic lifestyles, which set them apart from others. Yet, they were also sought-after and esteemed because people knew how much they could help the community. The figure of a Völva is often compared to the Veleda, the Germanic prophetess who was very respected among her tribe.

While there is little evidence of Seidr being widely practiced among men, it was considered an inappropriate activity for men in the Viking era. They had rigid gender norms, with men being associated with male roles like hunting and fighting in battles. This made it shameful for a man to adopt some aspects of female practices. Men who practiced this art were labeled unmanly (the common term was *ergi*), a great insult at the time.

One of the most notable reasons for ostracizing male Seidr practitioners was the weaving aspect of the practice, something only women were allowed to do. Despite this, some men still engaged in Seidr and even regarded it as their occupation.

The Tools of Seidr

One of the most indispensable tools of Seidr was the shamanic staff. While there is little evidence of its function, it is believed that the Sidr staff allowed the practitioner to focus on their intent. It also had a grounding effect because when set on the ground, it provided a connection to nature. It could attract nature's power and concentrate it. The staff could also act as a transportation tool when the practice included a journey.

Seidr practitioners often use herbs.
https://www.pexels.com/photo/white-and-brown-ceramic-bowl-1793035/

Other tools employed by Völvas and other Seidr practitioners were charms and herbs - which acted as protective agents during the practice. Shamanic work often involves connecting with spirits, but not all are helpful or well-intentioned. Charms could also be used for divination, along with runes. The Völvas were often depicted wearing a blue cloak, which they used to guide the souls of the departed to Hel. Freyja herself collected some of the souls, and the Völvas had the same abilities.

Different Levels of Consciousness

There are many ways to enter trance states, or "altered states of consciousness." Shamans and indigenous groups across nations believed this state was a bridge between the subconscious and spiritual realms. Being in this state enables the practitioner to connect more effectively with spirits and divine beings. Besides gathering wisdom and knowledge to use in life, it also helps them heighten their spirituality.

When you enter a trance state, you are neither asleep nor awake. Being in an altered state of consciousness requires you to travel through different levels of consciousness.

The 5 levels of Consciousness:

Level 1: Very Light Trance - It requires you to become more aware of your thoughts, feelings, and physical sensations. Practicing mindful meditation is a great way to reach this state.

Level 2: Light Trance - This is a dream-like level of consciousness that every person experiences without realizing it. For example, when you find yourself lost in thought while watching a movie, reading a book, or completely forgetting what you're doing, you're entering this state.

Level 3: Medium Trance - Also known as the "flow" state, the third level of consciousness is a little deeper than the previous one. In this state of consciousness, you lose awareness of the time, surroundings, and bodily sensations.

Level 4: Deep Trance - Most people enter into this state when asleep or falling into hypnagogia - a rapid and somewhat confusing state of consciousness that happens right before you drift off. It's caused by your conscious mind switching off and giving control to the subconscious. This level of consciousness is characterized by peculiar mental images and sometimes even hallucinations.

Level 5: Very Deep Trance - You completely lose consciousness during this stage, and it's described as being a deep, dreamless sleep. During Seidr, the most effective spiritual states are unlocked during the light, medium, or deep trance states.

A Seidr Cleansing Ritual

This simple cleansing ritual can be easily incorporated into your preparation routine for a shamanic journey. It uses juniper wood (you can substitute it for any other sacred pagan wood or herb). In ancient times, juniper was used for shamanic practices, cleansing, invoking spirits, or ancestral communication. The goal is to purify yourself from negative influences and have a successful journey. Besides cleansing yourself, you can also use this ritual to purge your home of toxic energies.

Instructions:

1. Gather your wood or herbs and tie them into a bunch to create a smudge stick. Alternatively, you can buy a premade one. Open your windows so the negativity can leave your presence as soon as possible.
2. Do a quick grounding meditation exercise using your preferred method. This can be listening to drumming music, repeating a mantra, breathwork, or anything else that helps you focus.
3. Light your smudging stick at one end and wait until it starts smoking.
4. Start moving the stick around whatever item, space, or person you want to cleanse. If it's you, envelope yourself in a smoke cloud. If it's your space, walk around in a clockwise direction, carrying the stick with you. Stop and linger at the corners, as negativity tends to collect in these spaces.
5. If you're using any tools before, during, or after the Seidr ritual, cleanse them by fanning smoke over them.
6. When you've finished, dip the stick into sand to extinguish it. Don't blow on it or use water, as this could offend the spirit you're trying to connect to.

A Safe Seidr Journeying Exercise

Before you start your journey, you must have an open mind, a clear intention, a quiet place to work, and a picture in your head of an entry point to another world. Additional tools like a blindfold, music, audio of drumming, and a stick (to act as a staff) may also come in handy.

Instructions:

1. Find a quiet space where you won't be disturbed. If you're inside, turn off your electronics and ask whoever is around to leave you alone.
2. Lie or sit down and relax your body and mind. Use the floor and not your bed. Otherwise, you may fall asleep instead of entering a trance.
3. Take a few deep breaths, holding each at the end of the inhale for 3 seconds. After, exhale until you've pushed all the air out of your lungs. Ideally, each inhale-exhale cycle should last longer than the previous one. Use your diaphragm to deepen your breath and make it last longer.
4. If you're using one, put on a blindfold. If you're uncomfortable using a blindfold, you can work in a dark room and simply close your eyes.
5. State your intention after relaxing your mind and chasing away all unrelated ideas. Make sure it sends a clear signal of what you want to achieve on this journey. At the same time, it should sound more like a respectful appeal than a goal you want to obtain at all costs.
6. Put on the music or drumming, and start focusing on it. As you do, visualize the entry point to the desired world and loudly reiterate your intention a couple of times.
7. Once you have the entrance in front of you, cross it. Be prepared to pay attention to your surroundings by using all your senses. You may see, hear, smell, or feel things. Don't be afraid to explore whatever channels have opened up to you; they could hold messages you want to explore further.
8. If you experience something negative, you can choose not to pay attention to it. If you can, retrace your steps or open your eyes to leave that world. The rest of the journey depends on your intention and purpose. For example, if you want to connect with an ancestral spirit or animal spirit guide, look for the signs of them reaching out to you.
9. If you're unsure whether you've encountered the right spirit, ask them. Or, look for four similar signs. If you meet four similar signs, it's a good indicator that a spirit is

communicating with you.

10. You can spend as much time on your journey as you like. However, the process can be somewhat overwhelming. Because of this, beginners should start with an 8-10 minute journey. Later on, as you become more confident in your practice, you can increase the time.

11. If you're using a shamanic drumming tape as a basis for your trance, choose the ones that signal the time to end the journey. If you're using music, select the one that lasts as long as you want the journey to last. Or, you can set a timer to signal when you should end your travels. Use a subtle alarm sound to avoid getting jarred out of your journey.

12. To come back, retrace your steps to the entry point. Walk slowly, memorizing your path in case you want to return in the future. This way, you'll be able to travel to and from that world with greater ease and efficiency.

13. When you've returned, stay still for a moment, and don't open your eyes yet. Reflect on your journey for a moment and stay grounded. Pay attention to how you feel - in your mind, body, and spirit. Does anything feel different than before your journey?

14. Reflect on the experiences you had and the messages you've received. Were you able to decipher them? Did you identify where they came from and what they mean? If not, you can write them down and revisit them later on. Sometimes, the messages only become apparent after some reflection.

Chapter 7: Utesitta: Sitting Out, Seeking Within

Utesitta translates to "sitting out" and is a form of meditation for anyone seeking stillness and answers to pressing questions by connecting with the Spirit. It involves sitting out in a natural environment, entering into a light trance, and performing acts of magic. In this chapter, you'll discover the origin of the Utesitta ritual and learn how it was used by the Völvas in ancient times. You'll also learn about the importance of breathwork and concentration for this ritual. Last but not least, you'll receive handy instructions on performing the Utesitta meditation and the breathwork that will allow you to focus during the ritual.

What Is the Utesitta Ritual, and What Are Its Origins?

Utesitta is an ancient meditation ritual commonly practiced by the Völva and other shamanic practitioners of the Norse religion. While there is very little information on the exact origins of this practice, it's believed that its roots lie in Germanic pagan traditions. The way Utesitta was practiced by the Norse shamans seems to support this belief. According to the lore, the Völva would venture into the burial mounds of the dead ancestors, sit on top of them, and meditate until they summoned the ancestor's spirit and obtained their wisdom. The Völva were powerful shamans and practitioners of magic, and they often ventured into divination as well. However, it's believed that most of the knowledge obtained by the Völva came from ancestral spirits. In essence, they used the Utesitta in the same way as they used runic divination. Whether they wanted to learn the outcome of a battle, decide whether to attack, retreat, surrender, or know whether the year's harvest would be successful, the Völva could consult the ancestors and obtain the answers.

In Uppsala, Sweden, archaeologists found burial mounds with a flat top, which suggests that they were built with the Utesitta ritual in mind. The work of the Völva was clearly visible from the bottom, and they could work comfortably. The Utesitta ritual often required a lot of time and focus, which was physically and mentally demanding for the practitioner. Sometimes, Völvas would receive requests from several people, who all sought answers about their futures. Sitting up on the burial ground, the Völva meditated until they found the answers that were hidden from others.

The Poetic Edda also references Utesitta in a poem about the hero Svipdagsmal. In need of some spiritual empowerment, Svipdagsmal sat on the burial mound of his mother. He meditated until he was able to rouse his mother's soul. She gave him advice and nine magical charms that would later help him on his quests.

Another example of Utesitta being referenced in the Poetic Edda comes from the poem of Voluspa. In it, a Völva is described using Utisetta to obtain a prophecy, which she delivered to the children of Heimdall. This particular foretelling included all the events that would happen in the world, including Ragnarok.

The Importance of Breathwork and Concentration

Utesitta is quite lengthy, which makes it rather challenging to maintain concentration. The longer you're sitting or standing focusing on your intention, the harder it is for your brain to exclude incoming thoughts. The same applies to the body - the longer you spend in one position, the more likely it will distract you by signaling you to move. This is when acquiring adequate breathwork comes in handy.

Moreover, Utesitta is not only about clearing your mind. It's about entering a state of altered consciousness - similar to a trance. In this state, you can connect to the other realms and speak with the deities, your ancestors, and spiritual guides. Breathwork can also help you remain focused on your intention of communicating with the beings from other realms and deciphering their messages, regardless of how long the journey takes.

The idea of breathwork is also tied to Odin. As one of the three brothers (half gods and half-giants) who created the world and people, Odin had an undeniable role in tying everything to the natural world. He was the one who breathed life into the three trunks the first humans were created from. It is believed that the Völva and other Norse shamans could connect to this life-giving divine essence through breathwork. Even nowadays, practitioners equate focusing on one breath with the idea of Odin giving life –and use it to empower themselves through Odin. They use this power to stay focused during Utesitta and harness the answers they seek.

Breathwork is a process of controlled and conscious breathing used to awaken your inner self. When you have control over your breathing, you can explore the subconscious part of your mind. It's a journey that takes you back to your core self. You can reach places beyond the realm of your intellect and awaken ancient memories - which promotes better spiritual communication during Utesitta. You can use your breath to awaken your spiritual potential, creativity, memory, and willpower for advanced visualization and communication. Through your breath, you can communicate with every part of your body to align it with nature's power and use everything around you to gain the wisdom you seek. Breathwork can also help you heal traumas and resolve emotions that could interfere with spiritual communication or hinder your ability to focus during your work.

How Does Utesitta Differ from Journeying?

The main difference between Utesitta mediation and shamanic journeying is the length of the practice. Seidr and other forms of shamanic journeying typically don't last longer than 15-20 minutes. For an experienced shamanic practitioner, 15 minutes is more than enough time to seek the required information. For beginners, it's also enough time to practice, even if they don't get answers immediately. Utesitta, on the other hand, is a much longer exercise. It can take hours or even days to complete depending on your experience level and the answers you seek.

Another notable difference is that shamans typically enter a trance-like state while journeying, whereas with Utesitta, you must stay right at the edge of entering this state to remain conscious enough to communicate with the spirit you're trying to connect with. Not only that, but you enter this state through a guided path. For example, you can listen to drumming and enter a trance to heal trauma or learn something from your ancestors. Or, you can journey to the spirit world and meet the spirits there.

The states of consciousness in Norse shamanism look like this:

- **Very light trance** - Achieved through mediation and simple breathwork
- **Light trance** - Used in Utesitta
- **Deep trance** - Achieved through shamanic journeying
- **Very deep trance** - Reached through guided shamanic traveling or magic

Utesitta Meditation in Modern Times

Nowadays, Utesitta is viewed as a spiritual embodiment of an experience of one's self as part of the natural world. There are many ways modern practitioners experience themselves as part of nature. One of these is finding a sitting spot where they won't be disturbed when practicing deep meditation. You can start with a simple 15-minute meditation to slow your breathing and calm your mind. Listening to natural sounds around you can help you with this. Feel free to return to this spot and do longer meditations. The more attuned you become to the place, the easier it will be to focus for longer periods in one sitting. Experienced practitioners perform Utesitta through the entire night - from sundown to daybreak.

Utesitta involves sitting still in nature.
https://www.pexels.com/photo/silhouette-of-person-raising-its-hand-268134/

Here is a testimony from a modern-day Utesitta practitioner:

"My journey began just before sunset, as the sun was dipping below the horizon. The night was quiet and cold, and the sky was cloudy. I sat in a quiet place, away from everyone else, wrapped in my cloak. After deepening my breath, I started traveling through the landscape and only stopped when I reached an ancient oak tree and the well beside it. I touched the charm that I wore around my neck. I let myself fall down into the well. While traveling downward, I was aware of the oak tree above me, but time slowly dissolved. I felt compelled to take a deep breath, and when I released it, I was standing on the ground, having resurfaced from the well. The sky was much darker, and I saw four crows flying eastward. Since my purpose was to reach out to the goddess Freyja, I started praying to her. I saw a picture of someone laying a wooden bowl under the oak tree, pouring mead into the bowl, and stirring it clockwise three times. They offered the mead to the goddess, asking for a good harvest in return. I read the runes etched into the wooden bowl and heard people chanting a beautiful song dedicated to Freyja. Focusing on this song helped me steady my breath and focus on my intention.

After some time, I felt the answer form. I saw myself standing in Freyjas's hall, feeling the pull to enter. I felt welcomed as I watched the candles burn. I knew I was between realms, and my answer was suddenly in my head. It felt complete, and I expressed my gratitude. I closed my eyes, and when I opened them, I was once again among the modern world, sitting in my secluded spot while the sun was about to rise." Chiara

Beginners are advised to perform Utesitta by following an experienced guide. Remember, this incredibly demanding exercise requires plenty of focus and willpower. Establishing contact with someone from another world can also be overwhelming, so you should always be extra careful about how you go about doing it. A guide can help you reach the desired state of consciousness safely and efficiently, so you can obtain the wisdom you seek.

Even with a guide by your side, you can't expect to dive into Utesitta immediately. Before attempting it, you should master effective breathwork and meditation techniques, which will train your mind to focus for longer periods of time and your body to stay relaxed for as long as required. After becoming confident in meditation and breathwork, you can move on to attempting to enter into a light trance. Practice this, as well, to get comfortable working in this state and see how you can use your natural powers while in a trance. Once you are comfortable entering this light trance, you can move on to doing an Utesitta meditation.

Nowadays, this in-depth meditation can also be performed for similar purposes as it was used by the Norse people in ancient times. You can use it to gain answers about future events from ancestors and spiritual guides or ask them for their insight about a particular situation. Sitting outside lets you reform your much-needed connection to nature and receive inspiration or guidance. Some practitioners use Utesitta as a channeling practice - to harness the energies of nature and the universe.

Many practitioners find covering themselves with a cloak or a shawl useful to block out visual distractions. Once the person resets their senses and blocks out distractions, they typically remove the fabric and look upon the world with new eyes. Their other senses will be heightened, which helps them enter a trance-like state.

Utesitta Exercises

Here is a beginner-friendly way to perform Utesitta mediation. It's designed to be done overnight, not just for a couple of hours. However, if you are uncomfortable doing it all night, feel free to reduce the time. As you're sitting in one place as a beginner, you'll probably feel compelled to ask yourself whether the exercise has a purpose. This is normal, but it just means you must train yourself to be more patient. It is something that happens to all practitioners. Everyone needs to go through that before they can understand the true spiritual meaning of the practice.

Preparatory Tips

Utsitta is traditionally performed on a mound or a faery hill. However, suppose you don't have mounds around. In that case, your ancestors' graves will work, too - especially if you want to communicate with their spirits. Before you embark on your meditation journey, think about your purpose. Establishing a particular reason for reaching out to the souls will help you obtain better results. Of course, you can go out and hope to talk to an ancestor. However, without a purpose, you won't answer questions - nor will you be able to focus on this quest for too long – plus you risk running into unfriendly spirits that can take advantage of you. Perhaps you're unaware of having any unanswered questions, but you still feel complete to try Utesitta. If this is the case, consider why you want to do it. That said, the question doesn't have to be too specific. Here are some examples of intentions you can set:

> *"I have a question I need to be answered, and I wish to talk to my ancestors."*
>
> *"There's a part of me that I fail to comprehend, and I need someone to provide me with clarity."*
>
> *"Someone has come to me with a problem that they need help with, but I don't know how to help them."*
>
> *"My pet dog is sick, and I need to know what to do about it."*
>
> *"I am here and would like to talk to you about..."*

Instructions:

1. Find a secluded place in nature and sit down.
2. Start paying attention to what is around you and how you experience your surroundings.

3. Look at the trees and the rocks. Observe the grass, the small animals, and the wind in the trees, and experience the sounds and the smells.
4. First, focus on one thing at a time, then move on to two, then focus on five things at once. The latter will be challenging, especially if you can't keep still.
5. Then, focus on your breathing, and bring your attention to yourself. If you're wearing a jacket, a cloak, or a hoodie, pull its edges closer to your body and put the hood on (if you have one).
6. You should now cease noticing anything from the outside. Concentrate on finding the core of your being. This could take 10-15 minutes to achieve and should be repeated for an hour or so.
7. Then, you can, once again, expand your attention outwards, except this time, you'll go past the boundary of your body. Try envisioning yourself experiencing your surroundings, but not as separate from you anymore.
8. At that point, you should become open to communicating with beings from other worlds.
9. You'll repeat this 5-12 times, depending on how many spirits you can reach and how long you're willing to seek answers or powers. Some entities will be less communicative, while others will readily help you.

Breathwork to Attain a Light Trance

Beginner Breathwork

To get into a light trance, you'll need to focus on your breathwork. Here is an easy way to get started. It's recommended to do this exercise in a sitting position. Avoid lying down, as having your legs firmly on the ground centers your mind during this. You want nature's energy to transcend your body and flow through it naturally.

Instructions:

1. Sit in a comfortable position and take a deep breath. While you're breathing in, count to four.
2. Count to four while holding your breath, and release it while counting to four again.

3. If you can, start extending the time while exhaling. If you cannot, stick to counting to four.
4. Repeat until you start reaching a deeper level of consciousness. You'll feel this when you sense your consciousness leaving you.
5. Let it happen automatically. Sit and let your breathing take over.
6. You should lose awareness of your body like it doesn't exist anymore. Only your soul exists - and it's now free to travel and communicate with other souls.
7. While the purpose of this light exercise isn't spiritual communication, if you encounter any other spirits, feel free to talk to them. If not, don't worry. For now, reaching the light trance is a perfectly acceptable outcome.

Heart Opening Breathwork

This simple breathing exercise will help you focus on your breathing and facilitate entering into a light trance.

Instructions:
1. Stand on the ground (preferably in a quiet place in nature).
2. Close your eyes and open your heart while feeling nature's grounding effects.
3. Take a deep breath and release. Repeat a couple of times until you're ready to visualize.
4. When ready, imagine a vast world in your mind's eye. This world is unseen to your eyes, but it slowly reveals itself to you.
5. Keep breathing deeply and releasing your breath slowly. Feel the strength of nature around you in the new world. Feel the life that flows through it all.

Chapter 8: Runic Magic and Divination

Runes are ancient symbols that had several purposes throughout the history of Norse Paganism - and this chapter will uncover all of them. You'll see how their use evolved from complex communication instruments to simple divination tools. You'll also find plenty of guides on selecting, consecrating, casting, and working with runes.

Examples of runes.
Pious Shy Boi, CC0, via Wikimedia Commons:
https://commons.wikimedia.org/wiki/File:Runic_Square_Font.png

The History of Runes

The information gained through historical records and Norse lore suggests that the runes were used predominantly as communication tools by ancient Germanic tribes. The earliest known evidence of runic writing comes from a carving that dates back to 400 C.E. When the Germanic pagans began to use the runes as letters (known as staves), they organized them into an alphabet. However, for the ancient Norse, the meaning of each stave wasn't as simple as the meaning of letters in most of today's languages. According to their beliefs, each rune symbolizes an aspect of life, a specific form of or a universal thought. The runes were used only by the most educated tribe members. They employed the runes to record events and prophecies affecting their community or to exchange information and forge alliances with the living and spirits.

In Old Norse, the primary meaning of the term rune is "enigma" or "a covert message." They believed that runes had magical properties which allowed people to send and receive messages from higher beings, inducing the deities, ancestral spirits, animals, and magical objects. The ancient Norse also believed that runes could unlock the secrets behind future events.

In the Norse alphabet, each rune was named after what it traditionally represented magically and spiritually. The earliest record shows that the staves were initially etched into stone tablets, which stood as a testimony to a particular tribe's achievements. As their knowledge of the runes advanced, Norse people began to inscribe them on small pieces of bone, stone, wood, or metal and carry them wherever they went so they could use them for different purposes. How each rune is depicted depends on how their name sounds and which letter they represent in the Norse alphabet. For example, the Tiwaz rune is shown as an upward-pointed arrow. This depicts the rune as the symbol of Tyr, the Norse god of war, known for his habit of traveling across the sky.

The runic alphabet is called "Futhark," which is an abbreviation of the runes Fehu, Uruz, Thurisaz, Ansuz, Raidho, and Kennaz. These were the first six runes of the oldest known runic alphabet, the Elder Futhark. This alphabet contains 24 runes, which were equivalent to a large number of letters in the Old English language. Elder Futhark is still used today for divination. The runes in this alphabet are divided into three Aetts, which are governed by three of the most powerful Norse deities, Freyr, Heimdall, and Tyr. Each aett also represents a specific stage in life - an early success, a failure, and prosperity in spite of life's hindrances.

The Meaning of Runes

The runes of the Elder Futhark have several meanings, often open to the reader's interpretation. That said, here are the aspects of life each rune is associated with, alongside their symbols.

ᚠ - Fehu

Pronounced "FAY-hoo," the name of this rune is translated as "cattle." Fehu can indicate abundance, material gain, wealth, luck, hope, property, and fortune. It can also symbolize the fulfillment of dreams and goals in the different aspects of life.

ᚢ - Uruz

Pronounced "OO-rooz," Uruz means "wild ox." Like this sacred animal, the rune is associated with willpower, strength, courage, perseverance, endurance, vitality, good times, and health. It is believed that Uruz has the power to shape one's destiny.

ᚦ - Thurisaz

Pronounced "THUR-ee-sazh," this rune in English means "giant." It symbolizes the hammer of Thor, protection, defense, disruptive forces, attack, or danger. Thurisaz can also mean that you must alter your life course to obtain divine empowerment.

ᚨ - Ansuz

Pronounced "AHN-sooz," the name of this rune can be translated as "revelation." It is associated with the Norse god Odin and his communication skills. Due to this, the rune depicts mental capacity, the mouth, and organs needed for speech. It can also symbolize other Norse deities you can communicate with through messages and insight.

ᚱ - Raidho

Pronounced "Rah-EED-ho," this rune means a "journey on horseback" in English. It can point to any form of movement, the conscious decision to work for your goals, progress in life, spiritual growth, and new perspectives.

ᚲ - Kenaz

Pronounced "KEN-ahz," Kenaz is a Norse term for ulcer. It can also mean torch, enlightenment, transformation, purpose, passion, or insight. Many see the rune as a sign of a higher calling toward following one's dreams. Kenaz can also mean you can't let outside influences affect your life.

X - Gebo

Pronounced "GHEB-o," this rune is translated as "gift." It's seen as a sign of gratitude or the need to exchange something through offerings. Practitioners use Gebo to obtain assistance, blessings, partnership, service, or luck through acts of generosity and charity.

ᚹ - Wunjo

Pronounced "WOON-yo," this rune symbolizes joy and well-being. It can mean the fulfillment of dreams and a state of contentment. However, Wunjo can also mean that your happiness may be threatened by an impending change. Through loss and tests of strength, the rune enables you to maintain the ability to grow and thrive.

ᚺ - Hagalaz

Pronounced "HA-ga-lah," this rune is translated as "hail." It denotes difficulties that could halt or delay your plans. It can also refer to external input or nature's destructive influence. Despite the latter, Hagalaz can change one's life for the better.

ᚾ - Naudhiz

Pronounced "NOWD-heez," Naudhiz means "need" in English. It can also highlight resistance, difficulty in thriving, lacking, or distress. It typically symbolizes the necessity to overcome a hurdle, the embodiment of your wishes, and the need to pay attention to your problems and unfulfilled desires.

I - Isa

Pronounced "EE-sa," this rune is translated as "ice." It symbolizes a hasty period of stillness when everything stops so you can see the changes you need to make. Isa is the key to successful self-renewal as it keeps you from following the same old patterns and remaining stuck.

ᛃ - Jera

Pronounced "YARE-a," Jera sounds almost identical to its English translation - year. This rune represents harvest, the cycle of life and nature, rewards for hard work, and the end of an era. It also symbolizes new beginnings, opportunities for growth, and gathering abundance and wisdom.

ᛇ - Eihwaz

Pronounced "AY-wahz," this rune is translated as "yew." According to Norse mythology, the yew tree embodies supreme wisdom. Its symbol represents ways to uncover the mysteries of life, connect to the sacred divine energy and knowledge, and find inspiration, stability, and stability.

ᛈ - Perthro

Pronounced "PER-thro," Perthro conveys fate, prophecy, mysticism, and the occult. It can also symbolize fertility, self-awareness, and new opportunities to raise your fortune. This rune is a hint that your future depends on your current choices.

ᛉ - Algiz

Pronounced "AL-geez," this rune means "elk." This animal is associated with good luck, protection, courage, and spiritual awakening. It's a cue that you must tap into your intuition to find the connection to your higher self.

ᛋ - Sowilo

Pronounced "So-WEE-lo," Sowilo is translated as "Sun." It embodies vitality, abundance, solace, motivation, and joy. Whatever obstacles you face in life, this rune provides reassurance that you'll overcome them.

ᛏ - Tiwaz

Pronounced "TEE-wahz," this means "the god Thor." It conveys all the attributes of this Norse deity - including boldness, leadership, honor, divine strength, and courage. It can also depict your ability to make sacrifices and thrive despite the hurdles you face.

ᛒ - Berkano

Pronounced "BER-Kah-no," Berkano is translated as "birch" or "the birch goddess." It is associated with rebirth, fertility, and new beginnings. The rune can also point to the potential for growth and finding creative ways to begin anew after a challenging experience.

ᛖ - Ehwaz

Pronounced "EH-wahz," this rune means "horse." In Norse mythology, this animal is the symbol of trust. Besides this, the rune can symbolize companionship, faith in your progress, and partnership. It can also represent animal instinct, needing help, or wanting to move forward with your life.

ᛗ - Mannaz

Pronounced "MAN-Naz," Mannaz is the equivalent of the English word "man." The rune embodies humanity, mortality, and the balance between life and death. It can also symbolize human values and skills you develop throughout your life.

ᛚ - Laguz

Pronounced "LAH-gooz," this rune has several meanings. Laguz is primarily associated with water and fluidity, inner awareness, the unknown, and potential. It can also denote dreams, imagination, and having an open heart even through difficult times.

ᛜ - Ingwaz

Pronounced "ING-wahz," this rune is named after the god of Ingwaz. Its meaning is tied to new beginnings and unveiling one's potential by harnessing new energies, ancestral wisdom, or using sexuality. It also embodies peace, well-being, and spiritual growth.

ᛟ - Othala

Pronounced "OH-tha-la," this rune means "inheritance" in English. It's associated with heritage, ancestral wisdom, nobility, homecoming, property, and hidden talents. It can also suggest that your values lie in your legacy and connection to your community.

ᛞ - Dagaz

Pronounced "DAH-gahz," Dagaz is a Norse term for "day." It embodies inspiration, the possibility of awakening, hope, balance, changes at the beginning of the day, and the beginning of a new cycle. It can also denote spiritual growth, happiness, clarity, and self-awareness.

Runic Divination

According to the Eddic poem "Havamal," the runes were revealed to people by Odin himself. He uncovered the runes and their power during his ordeal while spending nine days and nights hanging from Yggdrasil. After the ninth night, he looked down, saw the runes, and they told him how to free himself. Realizing that the runes held even more wisdom than he possessed, Odin shared them with the other gods and goddesses. He taught them their meaning and how to use them, and, in turn, they passed on this knowledge to the people.

Prophesying future outcomes with runes (the practice known as rune casting) is one of the easiest divinatory methods. Similarly to Tarot readings, the runes are tossed or laid on a flat surface and then interpreted. The runes can be cast either randomly or in a specific pattern, in which case each rune has a particular purpose. Runic divination can only get you answers to simple questions to help you get a clearer picture of your future. It's not fortune-telling, and it won't give you specific answers. While the runes can reveal different influences related to your inquiries, they'll never show you a specific time of the day when something will happen. The runes denote the gateway to your subconscious through your intuition. By tapping into your subconscious and using it to decipher the runic symbols in front of you, you'll be able to find the answers already in your subconscious.

In the olden days, the runes were symbols carved on small sticks made from branches of nut-bearing trees. Traditionally, the runes were cast randomly on a piece of white cloth after a small ritual. This entailed the rune caster saying a quick prayer to the gods or spirits they asked to help interpret the results and looking up to the sky while tossing the runes in front of them. They would then interpret the results according to their preferences and traditions.

Selecting Your Runes

Nowadays, you can buy pre-made runes and entire rune-casting kits. They can be made from stone, wood, or even crystals. Crystals carry their own intrinsic magical energy but can be infused with your power or that of nature. You can also make your own rune set. This will foster a stronger connection between your energy and the runes, making it easier for your intuition to pick up the meaning of the runes. Whether you buy or create your own runes, selecting the right ones is crucial for making them work for you.

Here is how to select your rune kit:
1. Place your hands over the runes and see if you have any reaction to them.

2. Listen to your gut - it will sense the runes you have some connection to.
3. If you feel drawn to the runes, pick some of them up (or all of them in a pouch or box) and try to feel their energy.
4. These are the right ones for you if you feel a clear connection to the runes.

Consecrating Your Runes

After creating or selecting them, you must consecrate your runes. This will help you connect with the runes before using them for divination. You'll need a strong focus to do this, so make sure you aren't too preoccupied with other things to concentrate on your task. Here is a beginner-friendly way to consecrate your runes:

1. Place the runes in front of you and a candle beside them on your altar or table.
2. Light the candle and focus on its flame while you take a few deep breaths to help you focus.
3. Pick up a rune, recite its name aloud, and pass it over the candle flame.
4. Repeat with the rest of the runes.
5. When you have finished, put the runes in a protective bag or box to keep them away from negative influences until you need to use them.

Casting and Interpreting The Runes

Here is a simple way to cast and interpret the runes:

1. Place a white cloth on your altar, table, or another surface you want to work on.
2. Formulate a question in your mind. For starters, ask questions that can be answered with a "Yes" or "No." These will only confirm what you already know in your subconscious - but will help you get the hang of listening to your intuition.
3. Take the bag or box of runes and toss the runes onto the cloth.
4. Look up towards the sky, and if you wish to call on a guide to help you interpret the runes, do it.

5. Then, look down at the runes and try to interpret their meaning. Try interpreting one rune at a time.
6. The symbolic meaning of a prophecy depends entirely on your interpretation. For example, Jera means "harvest," which can be interpreted as reaping the rewards of your work.
7. However, when it comes up, you'll need to wonder whether you're expecting rewards for any work you've done recently.
8. If the first thought you have when looking at Jera is that you're looking into a new opportunity instead of a reward - then this is probably the correct meaning at that time.

Reading a Rune Spread

Once you've mastered reading one rune, you can move on to a three-rune spread. Here is how to do that:

1. Take a deep breath, take out three runes, and lay them in front of you in a horizontal line.
2. The middle one reflects your current situation and actions.
3. The one on the left showcases past influences.
4. While the rune on the right illustrates the most likely future outcome of your present actions.

Creating Your Own Charms and Spells

While you can use pre-existing charms and spells, creating your own will make them even more powerful. However, to do this, you'll need to understand how the position of the runes will impact their effectiveness in a charm or spell. Here are the positions to consider:

- **Direct position** - Indicates their most indicative values and symbolism.
- **Inverted runes:** Related to the direct meaning of the runes but in a somewhat exaggerated manner.
- **Mirror position:** Use them to make bind runes, but exercise precaution because they have the power to trap energy and provide very little in return.

When making your own spells and charms, you must work on your visualization technique and sharpen your intuition as much as possible. Here is how to do it:

1. Visualize your intent until it becomes a word you can see in front of you. One simple word can be so powerful that it is enough to take effect. You can create rune spells or charms from composite words if you're more confident.
2. Alternatively, you can inscribe entire spells into your runic magical tool. For example, you can use spells for protection, fertility, or summoning guides.
3. Repeat visualizing the rune you're using until you can do it confidently. The easier it's for you to do this, the more effective your magic will be.
4. If you have trouble visualizing runes, pick one from a table before you and try to imagine it with your eyes closed. Try with black and white images first, then move on to colored ones.
5. When you've mastered imagining the runes' shape, you can add textures or images to their forms. Try finding images that best represent their core meaning, and focus on these when trying to visualize them.
6. Once you can connect to their core meaning, you'll be able to memorize the details you'll need when trying to create the runes that best describe your intention.
7. Next, depending on your purpose, select the material you will use. If you have a long-term goal, you'll need something sturdy, like stone or wood. If you have a short-term goal, paper will suffice.
8. Don't forget to consider whether you want to create a spell, a talisman, or something else. For example, if you're making a protective charm for yourself, you'll need to carry it around to take effect. In this case, you can create a pendant for a necklace, which you can take wherever you go.
9. However, if you need protection for your home, an art piece to hang on your walls would be a more suitable choice.
10. Carve the rune into the desired surface while sitting in a calming atmosphere. You can meditate beforehand to relax your mind and let it focus on the task.
11. You can also repeat the meditation when you have finished your work. Don't forget to thank your guides for their help.

12. Keep the rune somewhere you can see it whenever you need to draw on its power. Once you've reached your goal, you can destroy the rune.

Chapter 9: Bindrunes and Sigils

The use of symbols and sigils has been an integral part of human spirituality and magical practices for millennia. In Norse paganism, the use of bindrunes holds a significant place in both historical and modern practices. Bindrunes, also known as rune sigils, are symbols created by combining two or more runic letters to form a unique design with a specific meaning and purpose.

Historically, bindrunes were used in ancient Germanic and Norse cultures to convey personal or family identity, protection, and magical intent. For instance, Viking warriors would carve bindrunes into their weapons or shields to imbue them with the power of the runes and protect themselves in battle. They were also used in everyday life to ward off negative energies or to promote prosperity and good luck.

Ing bindrune.
https://commons.wikimedia.org/wiki/File:Ing_bindrune.png

Today, bindrunes continue to play an essential role in modern magical practices and Norse paganism. They are used in spells, meditations, and ritual practices to manifest intentions, protect oneself, and connect with the energies of the runes. Additionally, creating a personal bindrune can be a powerful tool for self-expression, personal growth, and spiritual development.

This chapter will provide an in-depth look into the intricacies of bindrunes and their significance in Norse paganism. Plus, you'll learn how to create and consecrate your bindrune using elemental energy and various activation methods. This exploration of bindrunes will provide you with the tools needed to create a personalized symbol of power that can help you manifest your intentions, connect with the energies of the runes, and deepen your spiritual practice.

Types of Bindrunes

Bindrunes are classified into different types based on factors such as the type of runes used, their design, and their intended purpose or function.

1. Overlapping Bindrunes

Overlapping bindrunes, also known as intersecting bindrunes, are a type of bindrune that involve overlapping two or more runes to create a new symbol. These runes are carefully selected based on their individual meanings and properties and are combined in a way that creates a new, more complex symbol with a specific purpose or intention.

One example of an overlapping bindrune is the Vegvisir, often used as a protective symbol in Norse paganism. The Vegvisir was created by overlapping several different runes, including the Othala, Algiz, and Isa runes. The Othala rune is a straight line with two diagonal lines branching off it, while the Algiz rune looks like a diamond shape with two diagonal lines branching off the top. Finally, the Isa rune looks like an upright straight line.

When these runes overlap, they create a complex symbol that provides guidance and protection to the wearer. Overlapping bindrunes can also be used for other purposes, such as healing, manifestation, and creativity.

2. Stacked Bindrunes

Stacked bindrunes, on the other hand, are a type of linear bindrune that involve the combination of two or more runes stacked on top of each other. This type is often used in modern magic and can be seen in various symbols, logos, and designs.

One example of a stacked bindrune is the modern Bluetooth symbol, created by overlapping the runes for "H" and "B" to create a new, more complex symbol. Stacked bindrunes are often used for specific purposes, such as communication, protection, or manifestation, and are carefully crafted to include the appropriate runes and symbolism for the intended purpose.

3. Linear Bindrunes

Linear bindrunes combine two or more runes in a linear fashion along the same axis. This can involve overlapping the runes or placing them side-by-side. When creating a linear bindrune, the specific runes used and their placement are important considerations. Each rune has a specific meaning and energy associated with it, and the combination of these energies can create a powerful symbol with a specific purpose. For example, the Odin bindrune combines the Othala, Dagaz, and Isa runes in a linear fashion. The Othala rune represents inheritance and property, the Dagaz rune represents transformation and new beginnings, while the Isa rune represents stillness and focus. When these three runes are combined linearly, they create a powerful symbol that can help the user manifest new beginnings and focus on achieving their goals.

4. Stave Bindrunes

Stave bindrunes, or radial bindrunes, combine multiple runes stemming from a common center point. This type of bindrune is commonly used for protection or as an amulet. An example of a stave bindrune is the Helm of Awe, which combines the Algiz, Raido, and Othala runes. The Algiz rune represents protection and defense, the Raido rune represents movement and journey, while the Othala rune represents inheritance and property. When these three runes are combined radially, they create a powerful symbol that provides protection and security to the wearer.

In addition, some bindrunes are designed to function as sigils, symbols charged with magical intent to achieve a specific outcome. The design can be personalized by combining specific runes uniquely and meaningfully while incorporating additional lines, curves, or symbols into the basic structure. The sigil bindrune is then charged with magical intent through various methods, like visualization, meditation, or ritualistic practices.

Sigil bindrunes are used in magic and ritual to manifest a desired outcome, like protection, success, or love. They can be created for personal use or shared with others to invoke a specific energy or intention. Once charged, the sigil bindrune can be used in various ways, such as drawing it on a piece of paper or carving it onto a piece of wood or stone. Some practitioners also carry the sigil bindrune with them or incorporate it into their personal altar or sacred space.

The power of a sigil bindrune lies in its ability to combine the energies of multiple runes into a single symbol charged with a specific intent. The design can be adapted to suit the specific needs and desires of the practitioner, making it a highly personalized and effective tool in magic and ritual. However, the effectiveness of a sigil bindrune relies on the focus and intent of the practitioner, as well as their connection to the energy and symbolism of the runes used to create it.

Crafting Bindrunes: A Step-by-Step Guide

Crafting your own bindrune is a fun and creative process that can bring a sense of empowerment and help you with specific rituals in your practice. Before you start doodling runes on a piece of paper, you need to understand the meanings of each individual rune. Mixing the wrong ones can lead to unintended consequences or even nullify the intended outcome. Don't let this intimidate you, though. The best way to learn is by doing, and practice makes perfect. Start with a simple two-rune sigil for a short-term goal, and don't be afraid to experiment. Look at other bind runes made by experts, analyze them, and see how they work. There are many runic alphabets to choose from, but as a beginner, the Elder Futhark is the most common one to start with. Once you've gained sufficient knowledge of runes, follow this step-by-step guide. Remember, the possibilities are endless, so let your creativity flow and have fun!

1. Visualize the Desired Outcome

Before you start picking runes, take some time to visualize what you want to achieve and the steps you need to take to get there. Once you have a clear picture of your goal, you can choose the runes that correspond to your desired outcome. Remember to pay attention to the meanings of each individual rune and how they can work together to create a powerful sigil.

Let's say you want to create a bindrune for success in your job search. The first step would be to visualize what success in your job search looks like. Perhaps it's landing your dream job, or maybe it's simply getting more interviews. Once you have a clear picture of your desired outcome, consider what qualities or attributes you need to succeed. For example, you might need confidence, communication skills, or networking abilities. Then, you can choose runes representing those qualities and combine them into a bindrune representing your goal.

2. Select the Runes

When selecting the runes for your bind rune, take some time to really consider each one and its meanings. This step is crucial as each rune you choose will impact your bind rune's overall intention and effectiveness. One helpful tip is to research the runes and their meanings. Take some time to understand the symbolism behind each rune and how they have been used historically. This will help you to make more informed decisions when selecting which runes to include in your bind rune.

You should also avoid over-complicating things. For beginners, it's better to limit your choices to two or three runes, and even for more experienced practitioners, it's usually best to keep it simple with five at most. This way, you can ensure that each rune you include has a clear purpose and contributes to the overall goal of your bind rune.

For instance, if your goal is to get a new job, you could select the runes representing success, communication, and prosperity. In this case, you could choose the runes Raidho (symbolizing travel and journeys), Ansuz (representing communication and inspiration), and Fehu (meaning wealth and prosperity). Together, these three runes would create a bind rune that focuses on finding success and prosperity.

3. Create Your Design

Now that you have selected the runes that best fit your intention, it's time to create your own unique bind rune. Get a pen and paper and start drawing as many combinations as you can. Don't worry about making mistakes; this is a creative process, and there's no right or wrong way to do it. If you're feeling stuck, take a break and do something else to clear your mind. Sometimes the perfect design will come to you unexpectedly, like in a dream or while taking a walk. When you return to your sketches, pick the ones that resonate with you the most. Take a closer look to see if any hidden or reversed runes have appeared, as these can affect the purpose of your spell.

Continuing the example above, you can create a design for your bindrune by creating a horizontal line with the Raidho rune at the left end, the Ansuz rune at the center, and the Fehu rune at the right end. Or, to add an extra layer of meaning, the three runes could also be positioned vertically, with Raidho at the top, Ansuz in the middle, and Fehu at the bottom. This arrangement can represent a journey toward prosperity, with communication and inspiration playing a crucial role in achieving success.

4. Select the Material

Choosing the right material for your bind rune is an essential step of the process. The material you use can have a significant impact on the effectiveness of the bind rune. When selecting the material, you should consider the purpose of your bind rune and how you intend to use it. If you are creating it for a long-term goal, it's best to choose a material that can withstand the test of time, like stone or wood. These materials have been used for centuries in magical practices and are known for their durability. On the other hand, if your bind rune is for a short-term goal, regular paper or cardboard can suffice.

When selecting the material, you should also consider how you plan to use the bind rune. If you want to wear it as a necklace, you can use a small piece of wood or stone and attach a chain or a string to it. Alternatively, if you want to hang it on your wall, you can use a piece of canvas or paper and create a beautiful art piece. Whatever you choose, make sure it's practical and easy to carry or display.

Consecrating Your Bindrune

Before you jump into the process of consecrating your bindrune, you need to learn more about elemental energy and its significance. According to ancient beliefs, the elements of Earth, Air, Fire, and Water are the universe's building blocks, and each of these elements carries a unique energy that can be harnessed for magical purposes.

There are various methods of activation when it comes to consecrating your bindrune. One way is to engrave or draw your bindrune on a material associated with an element. For example, if you want to infuse your bindrune with the energy of Fire, you can carve it on a piece of wood and then burn it in a fire to release the energy.

Another way is to create a ritual with elemental symbols and tools. You can use candles, incense, and crystals to represent the different elements and create a sacred space for your ritual. For example, you can light a green candle for Earth, a yellow candle for Air, a red candle for

Fire, and a blue candle for Water to symbolize the four elements and their energies.

You can also charge your bindrune with elemental energy through visualization and meditation. This involves visualizing the energy of the element you want to infuse into your bindrune and meditating on it. For example, suppose you want to charge your bindrune with the energy of water. In that case, you can visualize yourself standing under a waterfall, feeling the cool water washing over you and filling your bindrune with its energy.

Consecrating your bindrune is an essential part of the ritual in Norse Paganism. It is believed that the act of consecration imbues your bindrune with divine power and makes it a sacred object. By doing so, you're inviting the deities to bless and empower your bindrune, increasing the effectiveness of your spell.

Putting Your Bindrune to Work

Now that you have created and consecrated your bindrune, it's time to put it to work. Depending on your intention and creativity, there are numerous ways to use your bindrune. You can wear it as jewelry, carry it in your pocket, or hang it in your workspace. You can incorporate it into your daily meditation or place it on your altar. The possibilities are endless, and the key is to find what works best for you and your purpose. Using your bindrune consistently invites its energy and power into your life, creating a potent tool for manifestation and transformation. Here are some ideas that you can consider:

- Try creating a necklace or bracelet with your bindrune, and wear it as a talisman to carry its energy with you throughout the day.
- Draw or paint your bindrune on a canvas or piece of wood, and hang it in your home or workspace as a constant reminder of your intention.
- You can carve your bindrune into a candle and light it whenever you need a boost of energy or a reminder of your intention.
- Meditate on your bindrune, visualizing its energy flowing through your body and bringing your intention to life.

- If you have an altar or sacred space, you can place your bindrune on it as a focal point for your intention.
- Incorporate your bindrune into other spellwork, using its energy to enhance your spells.
- If you keep a journal or grimoire, you can include your bindrune in it as a record of your intention and a reminder of your magic.
- Create a small bag filled with herbs, crystals, and other items that correspond to your intention, and include your bindrune in it for added energy.
- Use your bindrune as a symbol in tarot readings or other divination practices, gaining insight into your intention and its manifestation.

Bindrunes and sigils are powerful tools in Norse paganism. They provide you with a way to focus and manifest your intentions. When working with bindrunes, the key is to select the right runes, design a unique symbol, and consecrate it properly, to create a powerful talisman that reflects your deepest desires. While this chapter provides a solid foundation for creating your own bindrunes and sigils, there is always more to learn and explore. Don't be afraid to experiment with different materials, symbols, and techniques to find what works best for you. Remember, the true power of bind runes comes from within.

Chapter 10: Stadhagaldr: Runic Yoga

Runes hold a sacred place in Norse Paganism, representing not just a system of divination but also powerful symbols of the gods and the cosmos. The Nordic tradition of runes is deeply connected to the primal forces of nature, the mysteries of life, and the spiritual realm. Over time, runes have evolved from their original use as an alphabet into a potent tool for personal transformation and spiritual growth. One way to harness the runes' transformative power is through the practice of Runic Yoga. Runic Yoga, or Stadhagaldr, is a fusion of yoga and runic symbolism that allows you to deepen your connection to the divine and unlock your full potential.

It involves using physical postures that embody the energy and meaning of each of the twenty-four runes of the Elder Futhark. Each posture represents a specific rune, and as you move through the postures, you connect with the energies of the runes, creating a powerful transformation within yourself. This practice has been used for centuries as a tool for spiritual growth. This chapter will explore the concept of Runic Yoga, its origins, and how it can be used to deepen your connection to the divine and unlock your full potential. You'll learn about the many benefits of this practice, the different runic postures, and how to practice it.

The Birth of Stadhagaldr

The origins of Stadhagaldr can be traced back to the 1930s, a time when interest in ancient runic signs was at its peak. Linguists, mystics, and practitioners sought to find practical applications for the ancient symbols. Two German scientists, Friedrich Bernhard Marby and Siegfried Adolf Kummer, believed that the runes were instructions for meditative gymnastics, similar to hatha yoga.

Marby and Kummer's theory even had a scientific basis, grounded in real archaeological finds, including the ancient German magical figures of *alraun*s, which were made as charms, and the sculptural images from the famous golden horns found in South Jutland. These images depict people in poses imitating particular runes, and it was the golden horns from Gallehus that inspired the development of runic yoga.

Marby believed that with the help of "rune gymnastics" or "rune dance," one could access areas inaccessible to the perception of an ordinary person, come into contact with higher forces, and influence cosmic processes. Kummer believed that runic magic allowed you to control energy flows from space by taking the correct runic posture and adjusting perception with the help of special sounds.

The name *Stadhagaldr* comes from the Old Norse words "*stadha*," which means to stand, and "*galdr*," which means to chant or to enchant. Although the use of certain poses, gestures, and the chanting of runes were not invented by Marby or Kummer, they rediscovered the forgotten tradition of Norse magic.

Stadhagaldr's unique combination of physical and spiritual practices makes it a powerful tool for personal growth and transformation. It is a significant part of the Norse pagan heritage, reflecting the deep connection between the Norse people and the natural world. Today, Stadhagaldr continues to be an important part of the modern pagan community, offering practitioners a way to connect with the divine and explore the power of the runes.

Benefits of Runic Yoga

The practice of Stadhagaldr is deeply rooted in Norse Paganism, reflecting the profound connection between the ancient Norse people and the natural world. One of the most significant benefits of Runic Yoga is its ability to help practitioners tap into the transformative power of the runes. In Norse Paganism, runes are regarded as sacred symbols that represent the primal forces of nature, the mysteries of life, and the spiritual realm. Through the practice of Runic Yoga, individuals can deepen their connection to these powerful symbols, unlock their full potential, and access hidden knowledge.

Another benefit of Runic Yoga is its ability to promote physical health and well-being. Traditional yoga postures are well-known for their ability to increase flexibility, build strength, and improve overall fitness. When combined with the transformative power of the runes, these physical benefits can be enhanced even further, promoting a deeper sense of connection between the body, mind, and spirit.

In addition to its physical benefits, Runic Yoga is also a powerful tool for mental and emotional well-being. The deep breathing and meditation involved can calm the mind and promote relaxation. This can be particularly helpful for individuals who suffer from stress, anxiety, or depression, as it provides a way to connect with the divine and find peace and balance amidst the chaos of everyday life.

For those interested in exploring their spirituality, Runic Yoga can be an excellent way to connect with the divine and explore the mysteries of the universe. In Norse Paganism, the natural world is considered sacred, and runes are seen as a way to connect with the spiritual forces that govern the cosmos. Through Runic Yoga, individuals can connect with these forces, gaining a deeper understanding of the universe and their place within it.

Another one of the unique benefits of Runic Yoga is its ability to connect individuals with their ancestral heritage. The practice is deeply rooted in Norse Paganism, reflecting the ancient wisdom and knowledge of the Norse people. For individuals who have a connection to their Norse heritage, Runic Yoga can be an excellent way to explore their cultural roots and connect with their ancestors.

Different Runic Postures

Runic postures are physical positions that correspond to the various runic symbols and are believed to represent the primal forces of nature, the mysteries of life, and the spiritual realm. Each posture is designed to activate specific energies and promote personal transformation. There are a variety of runic postures, each with its unique benefits and symbolism. Some postures are designed to promote strength and stability, while others are intended to cultivate mental and emotional balance. Below are some of the most common runic postures practiced in Stadhagaldr.

1. Fehu - Cattle or Wealth

The Fehu posture is a powerful runic posture representing cattle or wealth and is associated with abundance and prosperity. This posture can be performed by combining several traditional yoga asanas, including Tadasana (Mountain Pose) and Utkatasana (Chair Pose). To perform the Fehu posture, follow these steps:

- Stand straight with your feet hip-width apart, toes facing forward.
- Ground your feet firmly on the floor, and engage your core muscles.
- Lift your arms above your head, with your palms facing each other.
- Interlace your fingers, and stretch your arms up toward the sky.
- Inhale deeply and, as you exhale, bend your knees, and sink into a squatting position.
- Keep your arms stretched above your head, and continue interlacing your fingers.
- Hold the position for a few breaths, focusing on grounding and connecting with the earth.
- On your next inhale, rise up out of the squat, straightening your legs and lifting your heels off the ground.
- Hold the position for a few breaths.
- Lower your heels back to the ground on your next exhale, releasing your hands to your sides.

The Fehu posture combines the grounding and stability of Tadasana with the forward motion of Utkatasana to create a posture that promotes both strength and abundance. By sinking into a squatting position and rising onto the balls of your feet, the Fehu posture activates the energy of abundance and prosperity, helping manifest material and physical well-being.

The Fehu posture shares some similarities with the traditional Chinese practice of Qigong. Both practices combine physical movements and breathwork to promote physical and material well-being, and both draw on the ancient wisdom of their respective cultures.

2. Uruz - Aurochs or Strength

The Uruz posture is a potent runic posture utilized in Runic Yoga, symbolizing the primal strength of the wild ox and associated with vitality, courage, and passion. The posture requires combining traditional yoga asanas, including Virabhadrasana I (Warrior I) and Utkatasana (Chair Pose). Here is how to perform the Uruz posture:

- Stand straight with your feet hip-width apart, toes facing forward.
- Move your right foot back a step into a lunge position, bending your left knee at a 90-degree angle while keeping your right leg straight.
- Lift your arms above your head with palms facing each other.
- Inhale deeply and exhale as you sink deeper into the lunge, lowering your hips towards the ground.
- While keeping your arms stretched above your head, lift through your fingertips, and focus on the sensation of strength and power.
- Hold the position for a few breaths.
- Inhale and rise up out of the lunge, straightening both legs and lowering your arms to your sides.
- Repeat the posture on the opposite side by moving your left foot back a step into a lunge position and lifting your arms above your head.

By combining the traditional yoga asanas of Warrior, and Chair Pose, the Uruz posture creates a powerful and grounding experience that allows you to connect with the primal strength of the wild ox. This posture shares similarities with other yoga practices that focus on strength and stability, such as the warrior series in Vinyasa yoga. However, the incorporation of runic symbolism in the Uruz posture adds an additional layer of meaning and intention to the practice, allowing for a deeper exploration of the spiritual and energetic aspects of the posture.

3. Thurisaz - Thorn or Protection

The Thurisaz posture is a potent runic posture utilized in Runic Yoga, representing the power of the thorn or the hammer of the thunder god Thor. It is associated with protection, courage, and the ability to overcome obstacles. To perform the Thurisaz posture, a combination of traditional yoga asanas, including Virabhadrasana II (Warrior II) and Utthita Trikonasana (Extended Triangle Pose), are required. Follow these steps:

- Begin in a standing position with your feet hip-width apart and your arms at your sides.
- Move your left foot back three to four feet, with your left toes turned out at a 45-degree angle.
- Align your right heel with the center arch of your left foot.
- Inhale deeply, then exhale as you bend your right knee, keeping it directly above your ankle.
- As you exhale, turn your torso to the right, extending your arms straight out from your shoulders, palms facing down.
- Engage your core muscles and focus your gaze over your right hand, imagining yourself wielding the power of Thor's hammer.
- Inhale deeply, and as you exhale, reach forward with your right hand, extending it past your right knee and reaching toward the ground.
- Extend your left arm up toward the ceiling, keeping both arms in line with your shoulders.
- Hold the posture for several breaths, focusing on the energy of protection, courage, and overcoming obstacles.
- Inhale and straighten your right knee, then release your arms and step your left foot forward to return to the standing position.
- Repeat the posture on the opposite side by stepping your right foot back and turning your torso to the left.

The Thurisaz posture in Runic Yoga shares similarities with traditional Warrior II and Extended Triangle Pose in Hatha yoga. However, incorporating runic symbolism and intentionality adds a deeper layer of meaning and purpose to the practice, allowing for a more holistic and transformative experience.

4. Ansuz - Odin or Wisdom

The Ansuz posture in Runic Yoga represents divine communication and clarity of thought. It combines traditional yoga asanas such as

Tadasana (Mountain Pose) and Ardha Uttanasana (Half Forward Bend) with runic symbolism to encourage introspection and powerful communication. Here are the steps to perform the Ansuz posture:

- Stand tall with your feet hip-width apart and your arms at your sides.
- Take a deep breath in, then exhale as you bring your arms up overhead, interlacing your fingers and pointing your index fingers toward the sky.
- Inhale deeply again, then exhale as you lean to the right, keeping your arms straight and your hands interlaced.
- Hold the posture for a few breaths, imagining the breath of life flowing through you and filling you with inspiration and clarity of thought.
- Inhale deeply and return to center, then exhale and repeat the posture, this time leaning to the left.
- Release your hands and bring them back to your sides.
- Inhale deeply, then exhale as you lunge forward at the hips, keeping your back flat and your gaze forward.
- As you exhale, imagine yourself speaking with confidence and power, allowing the energy of the Ansuz rune to flow through you.
- Hold the posture for several breaths, then inhale deeply and return to the standing position.
- Repeat the posture a few more times, focusing on the intention of clarity of thought, inspiration, and powerful communication.

The Ansuz posture in Runic Yoga is similar to traditional yoga asanas like Mountain Pose and Half Forward Bend, which provide a grounding foundation while also encouraging introspection and communication. However, the addition of runic symbolism and intention-setting brings a deeper spiritual aspect to the practice. By incorporating the energy of the Ansuz rune, practitioners can connect with the divine and tap into their own power of speech and communication.

5. Raidho - Wheel or Journey

The Raidho posture in Runic Yoga is dynamic and energetic, representing life's journey. It is believed to enhance physical and mental strength and promote balance and harmony within both the body and mind. This posture is particularly useful for those seeking to embark on a new journey or make significant life changes. To practice this posture, follow these steps:

- Begin by standing with your feet shoulder-width apart and your arms raised above your head.
- Clasp your hands together tightly with your index fingers pointing upward.
- Take a deep breath and focus your intention on your journey, visualizing the path ahead of you.
- Exhale and begin to twist your torso to the right, keeping your arms and hands raised.
- Pivot your left foot on the ground to rotate your entire body.
- Hold this position for a few breaths, then inhale and return to center.
- Repeat the twisting motion to the left side, pivoting on your right foot this time.
- Focus on your breath and allow the energy of the Raidho rune to guide you.

The Raidho posture has similarities to several traditional yoga asanas, including the Twisting Chair Pose and the Warrior II Pose. Like these poses, the Raidho posture promotes strength, stability, and balance within the body. However, adding runic symbolism and intention-setting brings a unique aspect to the practice.

6. Kenaz - Torch or Illumination

Kenaz, the rune of torch or illumination, is associated with knowledge, creativity, and transformation. The Runic posture associated with Kenaz incorporates several yoga asanas that stimulate the nervous system and improve mental focus. This posture is often used to access deeper states of creativity and inspiration, making it a valuable tool for artists and writers. To perform the Kenaz posture, follow these steps:

- Begin by standing with your feet shoulder-width apart and your arms by your sides.
- Take a deep breath and raise your arms overhead, bringing your palms together in a prayer position.
- Inhale and lift your heels off the ground, balancing on the balls of your feet.

- Exhale and lower your heels, bringing your palms to your heart.
- As you inhale, extend your arms forward, keeping your palms together and your gaze focused on your fingertips.
- Exhale and slowly lower your arms back to your heart.
- Repeat steps 5 and 6 several times, allowing the movement to flow with your breath.
- As you continue to move, visualize the torch of Kenaz illuminating your inner creative spark and guiding you toward greater inspiration and understanding.

The Kenaz posture shares some similarities with traditional yoga practices such as Tree Pose (Vrikshasana) and Warrior I (Virabhadrasana I), as it requires balance and concentration. However, its unique combination of movements and focus on illumination sets it apart as a powerful tool for accessing creativity and insight.

Runic Yoga is a unique and powerful practice that combines physical postures, breathing techniques, and runic symbolism for personal growth and spiritual transformation. It is deeply rooted in Norse Paganism, reflecting the connection between nature and the Norse people. Through Runic Yoga, you can access the wisdom and strength of your ancestors, unlocking new levels of self-awareness and insight. The practice offers a pathway to a greater understanding of oneself and the world, unlocking one's full potential. The power of Runic Yoga should be honored and embraced for its transformative effects on people's lives. It is a potent tool that connects individuals to the divine power within and offers a pathway to deeper healing and creative inspiration.

Glossary of Terms

Asatru - A modern revival of Norse Paganism that focuses on the worship of the Aesir, the pantheon of gods and goddesses in Norse mythology. Followers of Asatru seek to connect with the natural world and the spirits of their ancestors through rituals, meditation, and personal devotion. It has gained popularity in recent decades as a way for people of Norse heritage or those drawn to the mythology and culture of the Vikings to connect with their ancestral roots.

Asgard - The realm of the Aesir gods, associated with war, strength, and wisdom.

Ancestor worship is honoring and communicating with deceased ancestors in pagan religions. It involves showing respect and gratitude toward one's ancestors by making offerings, performing rituals, and seeking their guidance and wisdom.

Alfheim - The realm of the light elves, associated with fertility, growth, and prosperity.

Blot - A ritual sacrifice or offering typically performed to honor the gods and goddesses in Norse Paganism. The ritual typically involves the sacrifice of an animal, which is then cooked and eaten as part of a communal feast. Other offerings, such as mead, ale, bread, or fruit, may also be given to the gods during the ceremony.

Eddas - The primary source of Norse mythology and pagan beliefs, consisting of the Poetic Edda and Prose Edda. The Poetic Edda is a collection of Old Norse poems that provides insight into the gods, heroes, and myths of Norse culture, while the Prose Edda, written by

Snorri Sturluson in the 13th century, is a guide to Norse mythology and poetic techniques.

Einherjar - The warriors chosen by Odin to fight alongside him in Valhalla. According to Norse mythology, the einherjar were chosen from those who died bravely in battle and were brought to Valhalla by the Valkyries.

Forn Siðr - Also known as Old Way or Old Norse Tradition, refers to the traditional religious practices of the ancient Norse people before the introduction of Christianity. It involves the veneration of deities such as Odin, Thor, and Freyja and the use of runes, magic, and ritual sacrifice. Forn Siðr is still practiced today by modern Heathens who seek to revive and reconstruct the traditions of their ancestors.

Futhark - The runic alphabet used in Norse Paganism, consisting of 24 letters divided into three groups of eight. The runes were used for writing inscriptions on various objects, such as weapons, amulets, and runestones, and they were also used for divination and magical purposes.

Gyðja - A female priestess in Norse Paganism who also leads rituals and provides spiritual guidance. Gyðjas were highly respected and highly esteemed for their knowledge, wisdom, and connection with the divine. They often served as healers, seers, and intermediaries between the gods and mortals.

Hávamál - A collection of Old Norse poems containing wisdom and advice attributed to the god Odin, often used as a guide for ethical behavior in Norse Paganism. It consists of 164 stanzas, each providing insight into various aspects of life, including hospitality, friendship, love, and honor. Hávamál also includes magical charms and spells that were believed to have protective powers.

Helheim - The realm of the dead, ruled by the goddess Hel and associated with death and decay.

Jötunn - A giant in Norse mythology, sometimes worshiped in Norse Paganism as a powerful and unpredictable force of nature.

Jotunheim - The realm of the giants, associated with chaos, unpredictability, and raw power.

Jörmungandr - Also known as the Midgard Serpent. In Norse mythology, Jörmungandr is a gigantic sea serpent, one of the three children of the god Loki and the giantess Angrboða. According to the legend, Jörmungandr grew so large that it could encircle the earth and hold onto its own tail. Jörmungandr was an arch-enemy of the god Thor, and their battles were said to be cataclysmic events that would shake the earth and the seas. In Norse mythology, it is said that during Ragnarok, the final battle, Jörmungandr and Thor would face each other in an epic showdown that would result in both of their deaths.

Landvættir - Nature spirits or guardians of the land in Norse Paganism, often associated with specific natural features such as mountains, rivers, or forests. They are often depicted as animal-like beings or anthropomorphic figures and were traditionally honored with offerings and rituals to ensure the land's and its inhabitants' well-being.

Midgard - The realm of humans, also known as Earth, where most myths and legends occur.

Mjölnir - The hammer of Thor, a symbol commonly used in Norse Paganism to represent strength, protection, and the power of the gods.

Níðstang - A pole inscribed with curses or insults, used in Norse Paganism as a way to bring shame or dishonor to an enemy or rival. The belief was that the curse would bring shame and dishonor upon the person targeted, causing them to lose social standing and respect within their community.

Niflheim - The realm of ice and mist, associated with darkness and coldness.

Nine Realms - The realms in Norse cosmology, including Asgard and Helheim, are inhabited by various gods, giants, and other supernatural beings.

Muspelheim - The realm of fire and heat, associated with destruction and creation.

Oath-taking - A solemn commitment often performed in Norse Paganism, in which an individual swears to uphold certain values or fulfill certain obligations.

Ragnarok - A series of catastrophic events that will ultimately lead to the end of the world. According to Norse mythology, Ragnarok will begin with a long and harsh winter known as "Fimbulwinter," during which the world will be plagued by natural disasters and wars.

Eventually, the final battle between the gods and the giants will take place, known as the Battle of Ragnarok. In this battle, many major gods and monsters will be killed, and the world as we know it will be destroyed. The god Odin will be killed by the giant wolf Fenrir, and

Thor will die after killing the Midgard serpent.

After the battle, a new world will be born, and the few surviving gods and humans will start anew. This new world will be inhabited by a new generation of gods and humans who will live in peace and harmony. In Norse mythology, Ragnarok warns about the world's impermanence and the inevitability of change and renewal.

Runes - Symbols used in divination and magic in Norse Paganism, believed to possess spiritual and mystical power.

Seidr - A form of Norse magic often associated with women, involving the use of trance, ritual, and divination to communicate with spirits and affect the natural world. The practice of Seiðr was viewed with suspicion by some in Norse society, as it was associated with the use of manipulation and deception to achieve one's goals.

Svartalfheim - The realm of the dark elves and dwarves, associated with craftsmanship and hidden treasures.

The High One - A nickname for Odin, one of the primary gods in Norse Paganism, associated with wisdom, knowledge, and the pursuit of power.

Thurseblot - A winter solstice celebration in Norse Paganism involving sacrificing animals and making offerings to the giants and other forces of darkness. This festival involves the sacrifice of animals and the offering of mead or other beverages to the Jötnar.

Týr - A god associated with war and justice in Norse Paganism, often depicted as a one-handed warrior who sacrificed his hand to bind the giant wolf Fenrir.

Valhalla - A great hall in Asgard where fallen warriors are taken in Norse mythology and Paganism, presided over by Odin and his Valkyries.

Vanaheim - The realm of the Vanir gods, associated with fertility, prosperity, and magic.

Vanir - A group of gods associated with fertility and prosperity in Norse Paganism, often depicted as having close connections to the natural world.

Ve - The brother of Odin and Vili, who helped create the world in Norse mythology and Paganism and may be associated with the powers of creation and wisdom.

Völva - A female seer or prophetess in Norse Paganism, often associated with the practice of Seiðr.

Yggdrasil - The world tree in Norse mythology and Paganism, believed to connect the different realms of existence and sustain the natural order.

Yule - A winter solstice celebration in Norse Paganism involving feasting, gift-giving, and burning a Yule log.

Conclusion

As you near the end of this book, try to reflect back on the rich cultural heritage of the Nordic peoples and their deep reverence for the natural world. This ancient tradition, steeped in mythology and symbolism, offers a wealth of wisdom and inspiration for those seeking to connect with their ancestral roots and find meaning in their lives. A quote by the renowned writer and mythologist Joseph Campbell comes to mind: *"Myths are public dreams, dreams are private myths."* In many ways, Norse Paganism is a reflection of this idea. The myths and stories of the Norse gods and goddesses are not just ancient tales but public dreams passed down through the generations, shaping the beliefs and practices of countless individuals over time. But, at the same time, the practice of Norse Paganism is also a deeply personal and private experience, as each individual seeks to connect with the gods and goddesses in their own way and to find meaning and guidance in their own lives.

One of the key teachings of Norse Paganism is the importance of balance and harmony in all things. This is reflected in how the Norse gods and goddesses embody light and darkness, order and chaos, and the cycles of birth, growth, decay, and rebirth inherent in the natural world. As you reflect on these teachings, you'll find inspiration to bring balance and harmony into your own life. Whether it's through meditation and mindfulness, cultivating healthy relationships and habits, or pursuing creative expression and personal growth, there are many ways to align yourself with the natural rhythms of the world around you.

At the same time, Norse Paganism emphasizes the interconnectedness of all things. From the intricate web of relationships between the gods and goddesses to the deep connections between humans and the natural world, people are part of a larger whole. In this spirit of interconnectedness, you should seek to cultivate compassion, empathy, and a sense of responsibility for the world around you. Whether it's through environmental activism, community service, or simply being kind to those around you, you can positively impact the world and contribute to the well-being of your fellow beings.

The study of Norse Paganism offers a fascinating glimpse into the rich cultural heritage of the Nordic peoples and their deep reverence for the natural world. This ancient tradition provides you with a wealth of wisdom. So, may the wisdom and teachings of Norse Paganism guide you on your journey of self-discovery and connection with the natural world. May you find balance and harmony in all aspects of your life and cultivate a sense of interconnectedness and compassion that extends beyond yourself to the world around you!

Here's another book by Mari Silva that you might like

Your Free Gift
(only available for a limited time)

Thanks for getting this book! If you want to learn more about various spirituality topics, then join Mari Silva's community and get a free guided meditation MP3 for awakening your third eye. This guided meditation mp3 is designed to open and strengthen ones third eye so you can experience a higher state of consciousness. Simply visit the link below the image to get started.

https://spiritualityspot.com/meditation

References

6 types of spirit guides & how to communicate with them. (2015, January 23). Mindbodygreen. https://www.mindbodygreen.com/articles/types-of-spirit-guides

Aburrow, Y. (n.d.). utiseta –. Dowsing for Divinity. https://dowsingfordivinity.com/tag/utiseta/

Aletheia. (2016, March 10). Scrying: How to practice the ancient art of second sight (with pictures). LonerWolf. https://lonerwolf.com/scrying/

Aletheia. (2018, February 5). 7 types of spirit guides (& how to connect with them). LonerWolf. https://lonerwolf.com/spirit-guides/

Ancient Roots, Historical Challenges. (n.d.). Pluralism.Org. https://pluralism.org/ancient-roots-historical-challenges

Anne C. Sørensen, R. M. J. H. (n.d.). Runes. Vikingeskibsmuseet i Roskilde. https://www.vikingeskibsmuseet.dk/en/professions/education/viking-age-people/runes

Ásatrú Definitions for Journalists. (n.d.). Norsemyth.org. https://www.norsemyth.org/2013/09/asatru-definition-for-journalists.html

Asatru Holidays. (n.d.). Thetroth.org. https://thetroth.org/resources/norse-pagan-holidays

Athar, K., Fey, T., Mabanta, D., Brian, P., Jackson, L., Damian, D. D., Scheucher, A., Paler, J., & Brown, J. (2020, August 21). What is shamanic breathwork and how is it used? Ideapod. https://ideapod.com/shamanic-breathwork/

Brethauer, A. (2021, September 10). Bind runes discover their simple and powerful Norse magic. The Peculiar Brunette; Amanda Brethauer. https://www.thepeculiarbrunette.com/bind-runes/

Byatt, A. S. (2011). Ragnarok: The end of the gods. Canongate Books. https://norse-mythology.org/tales/ragnarok/

Campbell, H. (2020, February 15). What is asatru? VikingStyle. https://viking-styles.com/blogs/history/what-is-asatru

Chambers, J. (2019, December 7). Ásatrú - Iceland's fastest growing non-Christian religion. All Things Iceland. https://allthingsiceland.com/asatru-icelands-fastest-growing-non-christian-religion/

Chris. (2022, July 2). A Complete Guide to Norse Gods & Goddesses. Panorama. https://panoramaglasslodge.com/a-complete-guide-to-norse-gods-goddesses/

Christianity.com Editorial Staff. (2019, September 23). Who Are Pagans? The History and Beliefs of Paganism. Christianity.Com. https://www.christianity.com/wiki/cults-and-other-religions/pagans-history-and-beliefs-of-paganism.html

Dan. (2012, November 15). Seidr. Norse Mythology for Smart People. https://norse-mythology.org/concepts/seidr/

Death & the afterlife. (2021, October 25). Skald's Keep. https://skaldskeep.com/norse/norse-afterlife/

Death and the Afterlife. (2012, November 15). Norse Mythology for Smart People. https://norse-mythology.org/concepts/death-and-the-afterlife/

Death and the Afterlife. (2012, November 15). Norse Mythology for Smart People. https://norse-mythology.org/concepts/death-and-the-afterlife/

Eliade, M., & Diószegi, V. (2022). shamanism. In Encyclopedia Britannica.

Estrada, J. (2020, March 11). How to use oracle cards, the simpler-to-read cousin of tarot that helps you tap into your intuition. Well+Good. https://www.wellandgood.com/how-to-use-oracle-cards/

Fields, K. (2021, December 29). Norse Magic: Seidr, Shapeshifting, Runes, & More. Otherworldly Oracle. https://otherworldlyoracle.com/norse-magic/

Folkvang. (2016, July 6). Norse Mythology for Smart People. https://norse-mythology.org/folkvang/

Glossary of Frequently Recurring Terms and names. (2012, March 1). Romantic-circles.org. https://romantic-circles.org/editions/norse/HTML/Glossary.html

Greenberg, M. (2020, November 16). Seidr magic in viking culture. MythologySource; Mike Greenberg, PhD. https://mythologysource.com/seidr-magic-viking-culture/

Gregg. (2010, May 23). How To Take a Shamanic Journey. Warrior Mind Coach. https://www.warriormindcoach.com/how-to-take-a-shamanic-journey/

Groeneveld, E. (2017). Norse mythology. World History Encyclopedia. https://www.worldhistory.org/Norse_Mythology/

Hel (goddess). (2012, November 15). Norse Mythology for Smart People. https://norse-mythology.org/gods-and-creatures/giants/hel/

Hel (The Underworld). (2012, November 15). Norse Mythology for Smart People. https://norse-mythology.org/cosmology/the-nine-worlds/helheim/

Helms, M. F. (2012). Valhalla. Createspace Independent Publishing Platform.

History of modern Paganism. (n.d.). https://www.bbc.co.uk/religion/religions/paganism/history/modern_1.shtml

How to consecrate runes. (2012, October 22). Allegheny Candles' Blog. https://alleghenycandles.wordpress.com/2012/10/22/how-to-consecrate-runes/

Jessica, S. (2019, June 3). Norse mythology afterlife. Norse and Viking Mythology; vkngjewelry. https://blog.vkngjewelry.com/en/norse-afterlife/

Lachlan, M. D. (2011). Fenrir. Prometheus Books.

Mrs, B. (2020, August 13). Intro to bindrunes. LunaOwl. https://luna-owl.com/2020/08/13/intro-to-bindrunes/

Nikel, D. (2019, August 21). Viking Religion: From the Norse Gods to Christianity. Life in Norway. https://www.lifeinnorway.net/viking-religion/

Nine Realms. (n.d.). Mythopedia. https://mythopedia.com/topics/nine-realms

Nomads, T. (2019, December 1). How to Make Your Own Rune Set. Time Nomads | Your Pagan Store Online. https://www.timenomads.com/how-to-make-your-own-rune-set/

Nomads, T. (2020, October 8). Rune Magic 101: What are and How to Make Bind Runes. Time Nomads | Your Pagan Store Online. https://www.timenomads.com/rune-magic-101-what-are-and-how-to-make-norse-bind-runes/

Nordic Wiccan. (n.d.). Blogspot.com. http://nordicwiccan.blogspot.com/p/httpnordicwiccanblogspotcom201404glossa.html

Nordic Wiccan. (n.d.-a). Blogspot.com. http://nordicwiccan.blogspot.com/2014/06/rune-yoga.html

Nordic Wiccan. (n.d.-b). Blogspot.com. http://nordicwiccan.blogspot.com/2013/07/runic-yoga.html

Norse pagan definitions. (2020, May 15). Skald's Keep. https://skaldskeep.com/terms-defined/

Northern Tradition Paganism: What is Rökkatru? (n.d.). Northernpaganism.Org. https://www.northernpaganism.org/rokkatru/what-is-rokkatru.html

Northern Tradition Shamanism: Utiseta, Breath, and Mound-Sitting. (n.d.). Northernshamanism.Org. http://www.northernshamanism.org/utiseta-breath-and-mound-sitting.html

Oddities, O. (2019, April 24). How to make a bindrune. Oreamnos Oddities. https://oreamnosoddities.com/blogs/news/how-to-make-a-bindrune

Oertel, K. (Ed.). (2015). Ásatrú: Die Rückkehr der Götter (3rd ed.). Edition Roter Drache.

Pagan beliefs. (n.d.). https://www.bbc.co.uk/religion/religions/paganism/beliefs/beliefs.shtml

Pat. (2020, December 8). The viking self and its parts. Maier Files Series. https://www.maier-files.com/the-viking-self-and-its-parts/

Pat. (2020, December 8). The viking self and its parts. Maier Files Series. https://www.maier-files.com/the-viking-self-and-its-parts/

Rode, B. (2021, April 13). Meet your spirit guide. Phoebe Garnsworthy. https://www.phoebegarnsworthy.com/meet-your-spirit-guide/

Runer og magi. (n.d.). Avaldsnes. https://avaldsnes.info/en/viking/lorem-ipsum/

Runes. (2012, November 14). Norse Mythology for Smart People. https://norse-mythology.org/runes/

Runes. (2021, October 26). Skald's Keep. https://skaldskeep.com/norse/runes/

Runic Philosophy and Magic. (2013, June 29). Norse Mythology for Smart People. https://norse-mythology.org/runes/runic-philosophy-and-magic/

SACRED CALENDER of ASATRU. (n.d.). Odinsvolk.Ca. http://odinsvolk.ca/O.V.A.%20-%20SACRED%20CALENDER.htm

Sam, T. +., & Wander, T. (2020, November 25). Rune Meanings And How To Use Rune Stones For Divination —. Two Wander x Elysium Rituals. https://www.twowander.com/blog/rune-meanings-how-to-use-runestones-for-divination

Sarenth, /. (2011, February 1). Stadhagaldr and breathing the Runes. Sarenth Odinsson. https://sarenth.wordpress.com/2011/02/01/stadhagaldr-and-breathing-the-runes/

Sebastiani, A. (2020). Paganism for beginners: The complete guide to nature-based spirituality for every new seeker. Rockridge Press.

Seidr Cleansing Ritual. (n.d.). Heathen Designs. https://www.heathenbydesign.com/seidr-cleansing-ritual

Shamanism. (2012, November 15). Norse Mythology for Smart People. https://norse-mythology.org/concepts/shamanism/

Shelley, A. (2023, January 9). Futhark Runes: Symbols, Meanings and How to Use Them. Andrea Shelley Designs. https://andreashelley.com/blog/futhark-runes-symbols-and-meanings/

shirleytwofeathers. (n.d.). Runic postures. Shirleytwofeathers.com. https://shirleytwofeathers.com/The_Blog/magickal-ingredients/runic-postures/

Sister, W. (2016, July 19). How to work with your spirit animal: A total guide. The Numinous. https://www.the-numinous.com/2016/07/19/work-with-your-spirit-animal/

Skjalden. (2018, March 11). Völva the viking witch or seeress. Nordic Culture. https://skjalden.com/volva-the-viking-witch-or-seeress/

Stàdhagaldr. (n.d.). Blogspot.com. http://galdrtanz-runedance.blogspot.com/2013/03/stadhagaldr.html

Strmiska, M. (2000). Ásatrú in Iceland: The rebirth of Nordic Paganism? Nova Religio The Journal of Alternative and Emergent Religions, 4(1), 106–132. https://doi.org/10.1525/nr.2000.4.1.106

Tetrault, S., & BA. (2020, March 29). What's the Norse, or Viking, afterlife supposed to be like? Joincake.com. https://www.joincake.com/blog/norse-afterlife/

The Meanings of the Runes. (2013, June 29). Norse Mythology for Smart People. https://norse-mythology.org/runes/the-meanings-of-the-runes/

The multi-part soul. (2021, October 27). Skald's Keep. https://skaldskeep.com/norse/soul/

The old Nordic religion today. (n.d.). National Museum of Denmark. https://en.natmus.dk/historical-knowledge/denmark/prehistoric-period-until-1050-ad/the-viking-age/religion-magic-death-and-rituals/the-old-nordic-religion-today/

The Origins of the Runes. (2013, June 29). Norse Mythology for Smart People. https://norse-mythology.org/runes/the-origins-of-the-runes/

The Self and Its Parts. (2012, November 15). Norse Mythology for Smart People. https://norse-mythology.org/concepts/the-parts-of-the-self/

The Self and Its Parts. (2012, November 15). Norse Mythology for Smart People. https://norse-mythology.org/concepts/the-parts-of-the-self/

Time Nomads. (2020, October 8). Rune magic 101: What are and how to make bind runes. Time Nomads | Your Pagan Store Online; Time Nomads. https://www.timenomads.com/rune-magic-101-what-are-and-how-to-make-norse-bind-runes/

Unrau, B. (2008). Scrying. CaltexPress.

Útiseta: The Norse Shaman's Wilderness Quest. (n.d.). Shanegadd.Com. https://www.shanegadd.com/post/útiseta-the-norse-shaman-s-wilderness-quest

Valhalla. (n.d.). Mythopedia. https://mythopedia.com/topics/valhalla

Vanatru. (n.d.). WikiPagan. https://pagan.fandom.com/wiki/Vanatru

What Do Pagans Do? (n.d.). Pluralism.Org. https://pluralism.org/what-do-pagans-do

What is deep meditation? Techniques & experiences. (2017, August 28). Mindworks Meditation. https://mindworks.org/blog/what-is-deep-meditation/

What were the similarities and differences between Anglo Saxon Paganism and Norse Paganism? (n.d.). Quora. https://www.quora.com/What-were-the-similarities-and-differences-between-Anglo-Saxon-Paganism-and-Norse-Paganism

White, E. D. (2023). Paganism. In Encyclopedia Britannica.

Who were the Viking Gods? (n.d.). Twinkl. https://www.twinkl.co.uk/teaching-wiki/viking-gods

Wigington, P. (2007, June 28). Asatru - Norse heathens of modern Paganism. Learn Religions. https://www.learnreligions.com/asatru-modern-paganism-2562545

Wigington, P. (2012, June 5). The Nine Noble Virtues of Asatru. Learn Religions. https://www.learnreligions.com/noble-virtues-of-asatru-2561539

Yggdrasil. (n.d.). Mythopedia. https://mythopedia.com/topics/yggdrasil

Yugay, I. (2018, January 15). Deep meditation - connection with your soul. Mindvalley Blog. https://blog.mindvalley.com/deep-meditation/

Yule. (n.d.). Thetroth.org. https://thetroth.org/resources/holidays/yule

www.ingramcontent.com/pod-product-compliance
Lightning Source LLC
Chambersburg PA
CBHW072154200426
43209CB00052B/1190